Water

Other books in the Fueling the Future series:

Fueling THE FUTURE

Water

Carrie Fredericks, *Book Editor*

Bonnie Szumski, *Publisher*
Helen Cothran, *Managing Editor*

GREENHAVEN PRESS
An imprint of Thomson Gale, a part of The Thomson Corporation

Detroit • New York • San Francisco • New Haven, Conn. • Waterville, Maine • London

For more information, contact
Greenhaven Press
27500 Drake Rd.
Farmington Hills, MI 48331-3535
Or you can visit our Internet site at http://www.gale.com

LIBRARY OF CONGRESS CATALOGING-IN-PUBLICATION DATA

Water / Carrie Fredericks, book, editor.
   p. cm. — (Fueling the future)
Includes bibliographical references and index.
ISBN-13: 978-0-7377-3593-2 (hardcover : alk. paper)
ISBN-10: 0-7377-3593-7 (hardcover : alk. paper)
1. Hydroelectric power plants—Juvenile literature. 2. Water-power—Juvenile literature. 3. Hydroelectric power plants—Environmental aspects—Juvenile literature. I. Fredericks, Carrie.
TK1081.W287 2007
333.91'4--dc22   2006030394

Printed in the United States of America

Contents

vegetation, which causes it to rot. The decaying plant material emits greenhouse gases linked to global warming.

Chapter 3: Can Water Power Meet Future Energy Needs?

Foreword

The wind farm at Altamont Pass in Northern California epitomizes many people's idea of wind power: Hundreds of towering white turbines generate electricity to power homes, factories, and businesses. The spinning turbine blades call up visions of a brighter future in which clean, renewable energy sources replace dwindling and polluting fossil fuels. The blades also kill over a thousand birds of prey each year. Every energy source, it seems, has its price.

The bird deaths at Altamont Pass make clear an unfortunate fact about all energy sources, including renewables: They have downsides. People want clean, abundant energy to power their modern lifestyles, but few want to pay the costs associated with energy production and use. Oil, coal, and natural gas contain high amounts of energy, but using them produces pollution. Commercial solar energy facilities require hundreds of acres of land and thus must be located in rural areas. Expensive and ugly transmission lines must then be run from the solar plants to the cities that need power. Producing hydrogen for fuel involves the use of dirty fossil fuels, tapping geothermal energy depletes ground water, and growing biomass for fuel ties up land that could be used to grow food. Hydroelectric power has become increasingly unpopular because dams flood vital habitats and kill wildlife and plants. Perhaps most controversial, nuclear power plants produce highly dangerous radioactive waste. People's reluctance to pay these environmental costs can be seen in the results of a 2006 Center for Economic and Civic Opinion poll. When asked how much they would support a power plant in their neighborhood, 66 percent of respondents said they would oppose it.

Many scientists warn that fossil fuel use creates emissions that threaten human health and cause global warming. Moreover, numerous scientists claim that fossil fuels are running out. As a result of these concerns, many nations have begun to revisit the energy sources that first powered human enterprises.

In his 2006 State of the Union speech, U.S. President George W. Bush announced that since 2001 the United States has spent "$10 billion to develop cleaner, cheaper, and more reliable alternative energy sources," such as biomass and wind power. Despite Bush's positive rhetoric, many critics contend that the renewable energy sources he refers to are still as inefficient as they ever were and cannot possibly power modern economies. As Jerry Taylor and Peter Van Doren of the Cato Institute note, "The market share for non-hydro renewable energy . . . has languished between 1 and 3 percent for decades." Controversies such as this have been a constant throughout the history of humanity's search for the perfect energy source.

Greenhaven Press's Fueling the Future series explores this history. Each volume in the series traces the development of one energy source, and investigates the controversies surrounding its environmental impact and its potential to power humanity's future. The anthologies provide a variety of selections written by scientists, environmental activists, industry leaders, and government experts. Volumes also contain useful research tools, including an introductory essay providing important context, and an annotated table of contents that enables students to locate selections of interest easily. In addition, each volume includes an index, chronology, bibliography, glossary, and a Facts About section, which lists useful information about each energy source. Other features include numerous charts, graphs, and cartoons, which offer additional avenues for learning important information about the topic.

Fueling the Future volumes provide students with important resources for learning about the energy sources upon which human societies depend. Although it is easy to take energy for granted in developed nations, this series emphasizes how energy sources are also problematic. The U.S. Energy Information Administration calls energy "essential to life." Whether scientists will be able to develop the energy sources necessary to sustain modern life is the vital question explored in Greenhaven Press's Fueling the Future series.

Introduction

Water is the basis of all life on Earth. All organisms, from algae to antelopes, require water to live. In addition to supporting life, water can be harnessed to power societies. Waterpower has been used for centuries to grind grain and power sawmills. In more recent times, the motive power of water has been tapped to generate electricity. However, despite humanity's long reliance on water for energy, water power is a source of much controversy. Like any other energy source, water has distinct advantages and disadvantages. While Americans can use the power of water to generate cheap electricity, they also want to protect the nation's lakes and rivers and the plants and animals that depend on them. These two opposing needs have become a source of intense debate in the United States. Much of the debate over waterpower concerns the environmental impact of dams, but controversy also exists over emerging water technologies that capitalize on the ocean's energy.

The Advantages of Waterpower

Proponents of hydropower—water energy created by dams—argue that it is a far cheaper energy source than is coal or natural gas. According to these advocates, hydropower is essentially free energy. Once the dam and other essential structures are built to convert the kinetic energy of the water into electric power, the water itself is free. Unlike the burning of fossil fuels, which uses up the fuel and requires that more fuel be located, extracted, and refined—water keeps flowing into the reservoir with the help of gravity and the weather. No strip mines, wells, or refineries are needed, thus minimizing hydropower's impact on the environment, advocates say. Moreover, water is a renewable energy source—unlike fossil fuels, which are finite and will eventually run out. Another advantage is that water emits no chemicals when used as an energy source—unlike fossil fuels, which emit greenhouse gases such as carbon dioxide when burned. Thus, proponents of hydropower call it a clean source of energy. As the Energy Information Administration, part of the U.S. Department of Energy, sums up, "Some people regard hydropower as the ideal fuel for electricity generation because, unlike the nonrenewable fuels used to generate electricity, it is almost free, there are no waste products, and hydropower does not pollute the water or the air."

Another benefit of hydropower is that the reservoirs created by dams can be used for a variety of purposes. Many reservoirs in the United States are used for boating, fishing, and other water sports. In addition to providing recreational opportunities, reservoirs store water for irrigation and for residential and commercial uses. Reservoirs also allow local authorities to control water flow throughout the year, which can help

Hydropower dams create reservoirs which are used for irrigation, recreation, residential and commercial uses.

prevent dangerous floods and make water available during arid summers. Dam proponents contend that reservoirs made possible the development of the arid western United States. Without reservoirs, they say, large cities such as Los Angeles would not exist.

Waterpower Also Has Drawbacks

Despite the many advantages of hydropower, several drawbacks have diminished its role as an energy source in recent years. One of the main disadvantages is the dams themselves. By interrupting the natural flow of rivers, dams disrupt fish migration patterns. Dam opponents point out that many once-abundant fish species are now listed as endangered as a result of extensive river damming throughout the nation. For example, in the Pacific Northwest, the dams on the Columbia River and its tributaries have greatly damaged one of the largest salmon fisheries in the world. The dams make the fish's annual migration upstream to spawn difficult or impossible, thereby reducing the number of young produced each season. Dams also damage surrounding river ecosystems. While hydropower proponents laud dams for helping to control floods, opponents point out that flooding is a natural and necessary occurrence. Downstream habitats depend on the nutrients delivered by annual flooding to remain healthy. The nutrients help plants to grow, providing more food for animals living near waterways.

Furthermore, while those in favor of dams claim that hydropower facilities do not alter the characteristics of water, critics disagree. They contend that damming a river changes the quality of the water that flows downstream from the dam. Water released downstream often has a lower nutrient load, colder temperature, and changed concentrations of heavy metals and minerals. Water altered in this way can have an adverse impact on fish, aquatic plants, and wildlife, they maintain.

The reservoirs created by dams also have an adverse impact on people, argue critics. Many culturally important areas have been flooded by the creation of dam reservoirs. For example, Glen Canyon Dam on the Colorado River flooded Glen Canyon in 1963. Critics of the dam argue that its reservoir, Lake Powell, has flooded the ruins of an ancient civilization, submerging important cultural artifacts. Dams also displace modern people who live near rivers. According to author Fred Pearce in his book *When the Rivers Run Dry: Water—the Defining Crisis of the Twenty-First Century*, "Dams have taken huge amounts of land—land on which people once lived. All told, at least 80 million rural people worldwide have lost their homes, land, and livelihood."

The Drawbacks of Hydropower Have Resulted in Declining Use

Because of these many drawbacks, hydropower use in the United States has declined. At its peak, hydropower provided more than 40 percent of the nation's energy. Today that number stands at less than 10 percent. As dams have become more controversial and hydropower use declined, scientists interested in harnessing the power of water have turned to other technologies. Many

Executives from Ocean Power Technologies, Inc. show an artist rendering of their planned Wave Power Station.

scientists believe these new technologies will accelerate the use of waterpower in the future. Wave, tidal, and ocean thermal devices are being developed to harness the immense power of the ocean. Since Earth's surface is more than three quarters water—most of it ocean—ocean energy is seen as an unlimited energy source.

Wave power devices, which float on the surface of the ocean, capture the enormous energy of waves to generate electricity. As the waves move under the cylinders, they rotate, turning a turbine. Tidal power uses the twice-daily rising and falling of the ocean water level to produce electricity. At high tide the rising water enters a chamber and acts as a piston, which pushes air inside the device upward, driving a turbine. The Energy Systems Research Unit, an energy research lab located in Australia, says of tidal technology, "If there is one thing we can

Wave power represents a virtual unlimited energy source.

safely predict and be sure of on this planet, it is the coming and going of the tide. This gives this form of renewable energy a distinct advantage over other sources that are not as predictable and reliable, such as wind or solar."

Ocean thermal technology takes advantage of the temperature differences between the warm upper layer of the ocean and the cool bottom layer. Facilities pressurize the warm water, which turns it into steam. The steam is used to drive a turbine. Then, cool water from the ocean's lower layer is used to cool the steam back into water, which is pumped back out to sea.

But controversies surround these emerging technologies as well. Building structures to withstand harsh marine conditions has proven difficult, with many installations breaking apart soon after completion. Large amounts of money are needed to build ocean energy facilities, and scientists find it difficult to find investors who will commit funds to such untried technologies. In addition, many people living near the sea object to artificial structures being built on or in the ocean. Such objects mar their view, ocean residents complain, and reduce property values.

The Future of Hydropower

Visions of these new water technologies supplying the world's future energy needs may or may not become reality. In the meantime, the existing network of dams in the United States and elsewhere will continue to supply the world with electricity. Despite the controversies that surround hydropower, it is still the number one renewable resource in the United States. According to the U.S. Department of Energy, in 2004 renewable energy sources provided nine percent of electricity generation. Seventy-five percent of that electricity was generated by hydropower. Whether that percentage shrinks or expands depends on how quickly supplies of fossil fuels decline and how viable other energy alternatives become.

A water mill along a stream. Water power is as old as human civilization itself.

CHAPTER 1

The History of Water Power

The History of Hydropower

Neil Schlager and Jayne Weisblatt, eds.

In the following selection Neil Schlager and Jayne Weisblatt explain that the movement of water flowing downhill creates usable energy. According to the editors, hydropower has been used for centuries. People have used waterwheels to grind grain, and today people build dams to generate electricity. Hydropower is considered a renewable energy source.

What Is Water Energy?

Water energy is energy derived from the power of water, most often its motion. Energy sources using water have been around for thousands of years in the form of water clocks and waterwheels. A more recent innovation has been hydroelectricity, or the electricity produced by the flow of water over dams. In the twenty-first century scientists are developing water-based applications ranging from tidal power to thermal power.

Historical Overview

The history of water energy is almost as old as the history of human civilization itself, making it the first form of "alternative energy" people employed. Many centuries ago the ancient Egyptians devised water clocks, whose wheels were turned by the flow of water. The Egyptians and Syrians also used a device called a *noria*, a waterwheel with buckets attached, that was used to raise water out of the Nile River for use on their crops. Two thousand years ago the ancient Greeks built waterwheels

Neil Schlager and Jayne Weisblatt, eds., "Fossil Fuels," from *Alternative Energy*, Detroit: Thomson Gale, 2005.

Water's power has been harnessed for centuries. Before the Industrial Revolution, farmers used water-powered flour mills such as this one to process grain.

to crush grapes and grind grains. At roughly the same time, the Chinese were using waterwheels to operate bellows used in the casting of iron tools such as farm implements.

The ancient Romans were especially skilled at managing water. In fact, the English word *plumber* comes from the Latin word *plumbum*, meaning "lead," referring to the lead pipes used in plumbing and reflected in the symbol for lead in the periodic table of elements, Pb. The Romans built water-carrying structures called aqueducts to channel water from natural sources to canals, where the water's energy could be harnessed by waterwheels. Near Arles in what is now southern France, for example, the Romans built a massive grain mill powered by sixteen waterwheels.

In the centuries that followed, until fossil fuels became the preferred power source during the Industrial Revolution of the nineteenth century, farmers continued to take advantage of the currents in rivers and streams for a variety of agricultural purposes, including grinding grain and pumping water for irrigation (watering crops). An English manuscript called the *Domesday Book*, written in 1086, listed 5,624 waterwheel-driven mills south of the Trent River in England, one mill for every four hundred people.

"Spinning Jenny"

Farmers, though, were not the only ones to use waterwheels. Early factories, especially in Great Britain and in the American Northeast, relied heavily on water power as well because of the large number of rivers and streams in the British Isles and in such states as Massachusetts, Connecticut, and New York. In these examples, rivers often powered such enterprises as sawmills, but the textile industry, in particular, used water to power the "Spinning Jenny," a cotton-spinning machine for making cloth. In 1769 English inventor and industrialist Richard Arkwright (1732–1792) patented a water-powered textile loom for spinning cotton (originally meant to be powered by horses) that revolutionized the textile industry.

But like many industrialists of the time, Arkwright built his fortune on the backs of his workers, who toiled from 6:00 in the morning to 7:00 in the evening. Among his 1,900 employees, two-thirds were children. While many other mill owners employed children as young as five, Arkwright was slightly enlightened for his time: he did not hire children under the age of six. Nor would he hire anyone over the age of forty.

The result over the next half-century was a boom in the textile industry, both in Britain and, later, in the United States. One of the pioneers in this effort was a New England businessman, Francis Cabot Lowell (1775–1817). In the early nineteenth century Lowell imported British technology to the

A tidal power station generates hydroelectricity. Although water power has been used for years, techniques for harnessing and distributing it have greatly improved.

Charles River in Waltham, Massachusetts, where he and other business owners built textile mills powered by the river. Later, Waltham's mill owners, needing more power than the Charles could supply, moved to an area north of Boston. Here they created the industrial town of Lowell, Massachusetts, almost entirely around water power. Soon, textile mills were able to produce millions of yards of cloth, thanks largely to water power.

The major problem with early waterwheels, though, was that they could not store power for later use, nor could they easily distribute power to several users. This disadvantage was overcome by the development of hydroelectricity (though modern waterwheels can also produce electricity). Hydroelectric dams, unlike waterwheels, do not depend entirely on the rate of flow of the water in a river or stream. Moreover, by producing electricity, power can be stored and distributed to more than one user in a community.

Hydroelectricity was first used in 1880, when the Wolverine Chair Factory began producing hydroelectric power for its own use in its Grand Rapids, Michigan, plant (perhaps it is no accident that the city had the word *Rapids* in its name). The first hydroelectric plant whose power went to multiple customers began operation on September 30, 1882, on the Fox River near Appleton, Wisconsin. Major improvements in hydroelectric power generation were made by Lester Allan Pelton (1829–1908), an inventor who is sometimes called the "father of hydroelectric energy." Sometime in the late 1870s Pelton developed the Pelton Wheel, a new, more efficient design for turbines that powered hydroelectric plants. A later design, developed by Eric Crewdson in 1920 and called the turbo impulse wheel, improved on the efficiency of Pelton's design. Because of these improvements, more and more electrical needs in the United States were being met by hydroelectric power.

A Pelton turbine generates hydroelectric power in Utah.
The Pelton wheel, developed in the 1870s, marked a major
improvement in hydroelectric power.

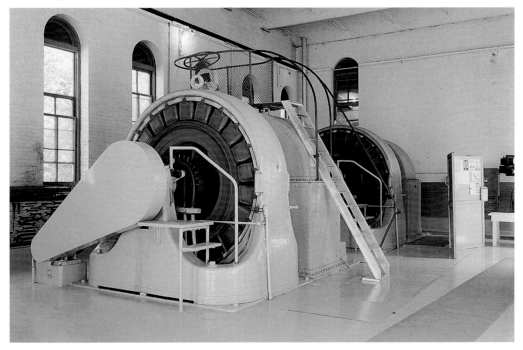

The water in rivers and streams, though, is not the only water in motion. The oceans move too, and in the late twentieth and early twenty-first centuries, efforts have been launched to tap the power contained in the oceans' tides, waves, and currents. Fundamentally, though, these sources of power are little different from the power provided by rivers and streams. The water is moving, so the challenge for engineers is to devise ways to convert that motion into electricity. While strides have been made, the practical use of these power sources is still in the beginning stages.

Energy in Tidal Power

Tidal power for electrical generation is relatively new. Currently, only one tidal power-generating station has been built and is in use. This plant is located at the mouth of the La Rance River along France's northern coast. The plant was built in 1966 and provides 240 megawatts, or 240 million watts, of electricity. There is a 20-megawatt experimental station in Nova Scotia, Canada, and Russia has a 0.4-megawatt station near the city of Murmansk. Other promising sites include the Severn River in western England, Cook Inlet in Alaska, and the White Sea in Russia.

Waves and ocean currents, like the tides, contain enormous amounts of energy, as any swimmer who has been pelted by a wave or swept along on an ocean current knows. The first patent for a wave power machine that would function much like a waterwheel in powering grain mills and sawmills was filed in France in 1799, although there is no evidence that the device was ever built. One of the first important developments for harnessing this power took place in 1974, when a British engineer named Stephen Salter invented a device called a "duck." This was a hydraulic mechanism that converted wave power into electricity, but this is only one of many ingenious innovations that scientists and engineers have developed. In the years that followed, scientists and engineers sought ways to transform innovations like the duck into a working wave power-generating station. Their efforts were finally successful in 2000, when the United Kingdom opened the first such station on the island of Islay, off the coast of Scotland. This station is called the Limpet 500, which stands for Land-Installed

Marine-Powered Energy Transformer. The number 500 refers to the 500 kilowatts of electricity it feeds into the United Kingdom's power grid.

The world's oceans are also the source of thermal energy, or the heat that oceans absorb from the sun. The word *thermal* comes from a Greek word, *therme*, meaning "heat," and is related to another Greek word, *thermos*, meaning "hot."

The first scientist to propose that the thermal energy of the oceans could be tapped for human needs was a French physicist named Jacques Arsene d'Arsonval (1851–1940) in 1881. D'Arsonval may very well have gotten the idea, though, from author Jules Verne (1828–1905), who imagined the use of ocean temperature differences to produce electricity in his novel *Twenty Thousand Leagues Under the Sea* in 1870. In 1930 one of d'Arsonval's students, Georges Claude, built the first-ever system for doing so off the coast of Cuba. The system he built generated 22 kilowatts, or 22,000 watts, of electricity. However, this represented a net power loss, because it actually took more power to run the system than it was able to generate. Then in 1974 the Natural Energy Laboratory of Hawaii Authority (NELHA) was formed. In 1979 NELHA successfully demonstrated a plant that produced more energy than it consumed (50-kilowatts gross; 15 kilowatts net). In 1981 Japan built a system that produced 31.5 kilowatts of net power. In 1993 NELHA set a record when it produced a net power of 50 kilowatts in a demonstration.

How Water Energy Works

To understand fully the nature of water energy, two terms have to be defined more precisely: energy and work. In everyday use, the word energy often refers to a substance, such as gasoline, coal, or natural gas. Strictly speaking, though, these substances are not energy; they are just chemical substances. Their energy is locked inside their chemical bonds, and it has to be released by burning them. What makes these substances useful is that they contain a lot of energy that can easily be released through combustion (burning).

Put differently, these substances can do a great deal of work, but scientists define work in their own peculiar way. To most

Multiple hydro wheels work to convert energy into hydraulic power to run a flour mill.

people, "work" means something like a chore or job, such as mowing the lawn. To a scientist, though, "work" refers to the process of converting one form of energy into another, such as converting the chemical energy of natural gas into heat used to boil water or heat a house. Scientists usually measure energy output in terms of the amount of work that can be done with it. For example, the calorie, used most often in discussions of diet, exercise, and weight, is actually a unit that measures a form of work. A more commonly used unit of work among scientists is the joule. The joule is part of the metric system units, and it is used to measure heat, electric energy, and the energy of motion.

To produce energy, though, it is not always necessary to burn something. When cleaning up after dinner, a family's first task is to rinse off the dishes, pots, and pans, using water from the kitchen faucet. What rinses the dishes, though, is not the water from the faucet by itself so much as it is the energy contained in the running water. This type of energy is called kinetic energy. The word *kinetic* comes from a Greek word, *kinesis*, which means "motion," so kinetic energy is the energy contained in a body of water when it is in motion. In discussions of water energy, sometimes the term *hydraulic energy* is used instead of kinetic energy. The word *hydraulic* is derived from *hydro*, the Greek word for "water." In this context, kinetic energy and hydraulic energy refer to the same thing.

Water in Motion Is Water at Work

To put water to work, then, the water has to be in motion. The best way to put large amounts of water in motion is to let gravity do the work. Streams and rivers, for example, flow because the water in them is moving downhill, even if only slightly, following the downward pull of gravity. In a home, water flows "downhill" because a city's water is stored in large elevated tanks, where it contains stored energy. When a homeowner opens a faucet, the water flows in a downward direction from the tank through the city's water pipes and out the faucet, where it carries enough kinetic energy to knock food remnants off dirty dinner dishes. Helping out is the sheer weight of the water, which pushes it down through the city's water pipes.

Scientists measure how much work a body of water can do using flow, which is simply the volume of water measured in, for example, gallons or liters per second or minute. This is just common sense. A homeowner who wants to rinse off a dirty porch uses a hose, not a squirt gun, because the flow from the hose is much greater than the flow from a squirt gun, so the water can do more work in a given period of time. A squirt gun might work, but the job would take a very long time.

This, then, is the basic science behind kinetic energy. Water flowing downhill, pulled by gravity, contains kinetic energy. A tool such as a waterwheel can be used to convert this kinetic energy into mechanical energy, which can then be harnessed to perform a task, such as grinding grain, sawing lumber, or running a textile loom. Or the kinetic energy can be transformed into electricity, which can be stored and distributed to many different users.

Current and Future Technology

The moon in large part is responsible for another type of energy that water can provide: tidal power. Every day, the moon (and, to a lesser extent, the sun), exerts gravitational pull on the Earth, causing the Earth's oceans to bulge outward. At the same time, the Earth rotates beneath this water, so twice each day, the Earth's coastlines experience high and low tides. These tides, just like rivers and streams, are water in motion. This motion, driven by the pull of gravity, imparts kinetic energy to the oceans. The ebb and flow of the tides along a coast, or perhaps into and out of an inlet or bay, are little different from the flow of water in a river, and they can be harnessed using technology similar to that used on rivers. Because the water flows in two directions, though, the system can generate power when water is flowing in and when it is ebbing out. However, a tidal power-generating station can operate only about ten hours a day, during the times when the tides are in motion.

The oceans' waves are yet another potential source of kinetic energy. Waves, which average about 12 feet (almost 4 meters) in height in the oceans, are caused by wind blowing across the surface of the water, just as tiny ripples are created when a person blows across the surface of a cup of hot chocolate to cool it. The height of a wave—from its peak, or crest, to its bottom, or trough—is determined by how fast the wind is blowing, the length of time it has blown in the same direction, and the width of the open water over which it is blowing. The steepest and most powerful waves are caused by winds that blow strongly in the same direction across oceans, such as the trade winds.

Waves move across the waters of the open ocean with little change. But as they approach the shore and the water gets shallower, they begin to release their enormous energy. First, the ocean's floor causes the wave to slow and to increase in height.

Waves pack an enormous amount of power. They release their energy as they get closer to the shore.

Then, the front of the wave "breaks," or collapses, hurling tons of water at the coastline. The force of this wave power is so great that it continues to wash away the coastlines. It is estimated, for example, that parts of Cape Cod are eroding at a rate of 3 feet (0.9 meter) per year. Like the water in rivers and streams, these waves could potentially be used for their kinetic energy.

A final source of kinetic energy in the oceans is their currents. Currents, like waves, are usually propelled by the wind blowing across the surface. The wind has to be strong and consistent. But other currents are formed by differences in water temperature and salinity (salt content) and even by slight differences in the elevation of the sea's surface. The currents follow paths determined by the Coriolis effect, or the effect of the Earth's rotation. In the Northern Hemisphere, the Earth's rotation deflects the currents into a clockwise rotation; in the Southern Hemisphere, the currents flow counterclockwise.

One of the most studied and well-known ocean currents is the Gulf Stream, which originates near Florida, crosses the Atlantic Ocean, and warms much of northern Europe. The Gulf Stream is 50 miles (80 kilometers) wide, and an estimated 10 cubic miles (16 cubic kilometers) of water move through it every hour. It moves so fast that its warm waters do not mix with the colder water that surrounds it. The Gulf Stream is, in effect, a river. The water is in motion, so it contains vast amounts of kinetic energy that could be tapped for human use.

There is also thermal energy, or the heat contained in the world's oceans. Tapping the oceans' thermal energy, though, is not just a matter of somehow going out and piping in the heat. The process, called ocean thermal energy conversion (OTEC), is driven by the ocean's thermal gradient, which refers to the differences in temperature between the ocean's layers of water. Power can be produced when the difference between the warmer surface waters and the colder deep waters is at least 36°F (20°C). Energy-producing systems for tapping the ocean's thermal energy rely on a system of condensers, evaporators, and turbines to generate electricity. OTEC could provide electricity, especially to many tropical nations that currently have to import all their fuel.

Benefits of Water Energy

The major benefit that all forms of water energy have is that they provide power without burning fossil fuels. Energy can be provided for human use without having to tear up the land to mine coal or disrupt ecosystems to drill for oil. The power they provide is clean—it does not release particulate matter, carbon dioxide, or sulfur dioxide into the air, contributing to smog and the ill health effects that smog can cause, such as lung disease. Also, because water energy does not depend on the burning of fossil fuels, it does not contribute to global warming, caused by the buildup of gases such as carbon dioxide in the atmosphere. Nor does it contribute to acid rain, or precipitation that is more acidic than normal because it contains such substances as sulfur dioxide. Acid rain, like any acidic sub-

The Volzhskaya hydroelectric power plant provides clean, renewable energy for Russian residents.

stance, can have harmful effects on forests, wildlife, and even structures built by people.

Another major benefit of water energy is that it is virtually inexhaustible. Once fossil fuels run out, they are gone. There is no way to somehow manufacture more oil or natural gas. However, the energy provided by water will be there as long as the sun shines and as long as the Earth contains oceans and rivers.

Further, the energy provided by water is essentially free—once, of course, the technology is put in place to extract the energy. While money would continue to have to be spent to build plants, maintain them, and distribute the power they produce, a major benefit is that power providers would not have to buy fuel for them. The potential savings is huge. As of mid-2005 the cost of a barrel of oil was hovering around $60. The United States uses about twenty million barrels of oil each day. That means about $1.2 billion per day is spent for just that one form of fuel. Replacing that fuel with water energy would result in enormous savings for consumers.

Drawbacks of Water Energy

These energy sources, though, are not without their drawbacks. While hydroelectric dams have been around for well over a century, stations for harvesting tidal, wave, ocean current, and ocean thermal power are still in the developmental stages. Exploiting these forms of power would require a huge investment. The cost of building a tidal power-generating station, for example, could run as high as $15 billion.

A second drawback is that water energy is not totally reliable. In an energy plant that burns fossil fuels, the fuel can be fed into the system at a constant rate. As a result, the energy output of the system can be predicted and maintained at a steady pace. Water energy can be a little more variable. In a dry season, the water in a river may not run as fast. The level of the water in the reservoir behind a hydroelectric dam may fall so far that the dam's operators have to slow the flow of water over the dam, cutting power output. In the case of ocean energy, plant operators have no control over the water. Tidal power, for example, can vary from day to day, depending on the alignment of the Earth with the sun and the moon. Wave power could be highly variable, depending on prevailing winds. While the power in ocean currents and in the ocean's thermal gradient is more predictable, the chief obstacle is getting to it. Creating a power plant in the middle of the Gulf Stream would be no easy feat.

A related problem is that water energy is not evenly distributed across the Earth. Providing tidal power to the residents of Nebraska would be impractical because Nebraska is nowhere near an ocean. While tides operate throughout the world, not every coastal region can produce tidal power very efficiently. Some coastal regions have higher tides than others, usually because of some geographical feature, such as bays and inlets that push the water to a higher level than it would otherwise reach. To be practical, efforts to harness tidal power require a difference of about 16 feet (5 meters) between high and low tide. This difference can be found at only about forty places around the world. As the water flows in, and then as it flows out, it can be harnessed in much the same way that the water in any river can be harnessed. However, tidal power stations would be possible only in a limited number of locations.

The use of river power, too, is highly variable. While hydroelectric power provides 24 percent of the electricity used worldwide and 9 to 10 percent used in the United States, much of that hydroelectric power is concentrated in regions with several rivers. In the United States, for example, 14 percent of the power used in the Rocky Mountain states comes from hydroelectric dams; in the Pacific Northwest, in contrast, some 65 percent of power demand is filled by 58 hydroelectric dams. While hydroelectric dams provide almost all of the electricity in Norway, 83 percent in Iceland, 67 percent in Austria, and 60 percent in Canada, they can provide little or none in the desert countries of the Middle East or in most of Africa. This suggests that no one source can magically solve any nation's energy problems.

A final drawback is that a fossil fuel-fired plant can be built essentially anywhere because the fuel is brought to the plant. With water energy, the plant has to be brought to the fuel, meaning that plants have to be built on rivers, along shorelines, and in bays, where they disrupt the natural environment.

Environmental Impacts of Water Energy

A major drawback to the use of water energy is the potential environmental impact. On one level, using water energy would have benefits for the environment, including cleaner air and reduced global warming, compared to the use of fossil fuels. However, the power plants themselves could potentially have a devastating effect on local ecosystems.

Dams, such as this one on the Colorado river, can drastically change a river's ecosystem and take up large pieces of land.

Hydroelectric dams are a good example. Throughout the world, about 40,000 large dams are in use to provide hydroelectric power. Most of these dams were built with little regard to the environmental impact they would have. Dams, for example, require reservoirs. In effect, they turn a river ecosystem into a lake ecosystem, at the same time gobbling up large tracts of land. Moreover, they block the migration of fish, such as salmon in the Pacific Northwest. They also prevent the downstream movement of silt, which is often rich in nutrients.

Such facilities as tidal power-generating stations could have similar environmental impacts. The construction and operation of such facilities could have a serious impact on marine and coastal ecosystems, fisheries, and the like. They could disturb the silt on the ocean bed, with unintended consequences. Further, they could convert beautiful natural areas into eyesores.

Another potential drawback to hydroelectric dams—or any water energy project—concerns ownership rights. Rivers usually flow through more than one country. In Southeast Asia, for example, six countries make up the Mekong River's watershed. During rainy seasons this would not be a problem, for the Mekong flows at a rate of 31 cubic miles (50,000 cubic meters) per second. During the dry season, however, the river flows at a rate of only about 1.2 cubic miles (2,000 cubic meters) per second, seriously reducing the amount of power that could be produced. This would provide an upriver country with an incentive to block the flow of the river, denying water and power to the downriver countries. The result could be serious regional conflict over water rights. A similar problem could occur in the oceans. It is an established principle that no country owns the oceans in its vicinity, other than a narrow strip along the coastline. Any type of power-generating station that lies outside of a nation's coastal waters would run into serious legal difficulties if it used international seas to provide power for just one nation.

Economic Impact of Water Energy

The economic impact of water energy has always been great, but new forms have the potential to dwarf the impact that has been felt throughout human history. While water power has been used throughout much of history, its economic impact began to be felt more fully in the late eighteenth and early nineteenth centuries. The town of Lowell, Massachusetts, which grew as textile firms built up around the availability of water power, by the mid-1830s boasted 20 textile mills employing 8,000 people and producing 50 million yards (46 million meters) of cloth per year.

Hydroelectricity had an even larger impact. In the early twenty-first century hydroelectric dams provide about 9 to 10 percent of the electricity used in the United States. Worldwide, though, hydroelectric plants provide about 24 percent of electricity, serving a billion people. Together, they annually produce about 675,000 megawatts (*mega-*, meaning "million"), the equivalent of about 3.6 billion barrels of oil. That represents a savings of about $180 billion that might otherwise be spent on oil. These hydroelectric plants are the world's single largest source of renewable energy.

Other sources of water energy hold even greater promise. Just over 70 percent of the Earth's surface is covered by oceans. The amount of water they contain is staggering: 328 million cubic miles (527 million cubic kilometers), or 361.2 quintillion gallons (1,367.3 quintillion liters). (A quintillion is 1,000,000,000,000,000,000.) Every day the sun shines on these oceans, and every day they absorb a great deal of thermal energy. In fact, the oceans can be thought of as the world's single largest solar panel. It is estimated that on a typical day, about 23 million square miles (60 million square kilometers) of the world's tropical oceans absorb an amount of energy from the sun equal to about 250 billion barrels of oil.

To put that figure in perspective, the total amount of oil produced in the world each day in 2005 was about 76 million barrels. That means that each day, the tropical oceans absorb three thousand times more energy than that provided by oil. This is an enormous amount of energy. Some experts estimate that the amount of power that could potentially be produced from heat in the oceans is 10 trillion watts. Just 1/200th of one percent of this thermal energy—absorbed by the tropical oceans in just one day—could provide all the electricity consumed in the entire United States. This energy would be clean and endlessly renewable. The problem, of course, is finding ways to capture that energy.

Societal Impact of Water Energy

The societal impact of water energy is essentially the same as the impact of any alternative energy. Clean, renewable energy would lessen the adverse health effects of fossil fuel burning. Because the fuel itself is essentially free, more reliance on water power would free up billions of dollars that could be used for other human needs. Using water power would also benefit the environment, reducing the need for environmentally disruptive coal mining and oil drilling, along with the regular oil spills that spoil many nations' coastlines. Water power could also have a major impact on poorer nations, which lack the resources to import fossil fuels for economic development. Water energy could provide these nations with a clean, relatively inexpensive way to develop and provide a richer economic, social, educational, and cultural future for their peoples.

How Hydropower Developed in the United States

U.S. Bureau of Reclamation

The U.S. Bureau of Reclamation reports in this selection that hydropower was developed in the United States to help build dams in the arid west. The dams allowed western states to manage water for drinking and irrigation. Water was used to generate electricity for dam construction activities such as moving stones, powering sawmills, and providing illumination for night operations. Surplus power was sold to local utilities, generating revenue for dam construction. Soon, the dams were used to supply electricity for general power needs throughout the nation. According to the bureau, the hydropower industry expanded to provide almost one-third of the country's energy needs. Today, hydropower provides only about one-tenth of America's power needs. The U.S. Bureau of Reclamation, a federal government organization established in 1902, is the second largest provider of hydroelectric power in the United States.

By using water for power generation, people have worked with nature to achieve a better lifestyle. The mechanical power of falling water is an age-old tool. It was used by the Greeks to turn water wheels for grinding wheat into flour, more than 2,000 years ago. In the 1700s mechanical hydropower was used extensively for milling and pumping. By the early 1900s, hydroelectric power accounted for more than 40 percent of the

U.S. Bureau of Reclamation, "The History of Hydropower Development in the United States," October 2004. www.usbr.gov.

United States' supply of electricity. In the 1940s hydropower provided about 75 percent of all the electricity consumed in the West and Pacific Northwest, and about one-third of the total United States' electrical energy. With the increase in development of other forms of electric power generation, hydropower's percentage has slowly declined and today provides about one tenth of the United States' electricity.

Niagara Falls was the first of the American hydroelectric power sites developed for major generation and is still a source of electric power today. The early hydroelectric plants were direct

The Robert Moses power plant at Niagara Falls, New York, was the first major hydroelectric power site developed in the United States.

current stations built to power arc and incandescent lighting during the period from about 1880 to 1895. When the electric motor came into being the demand for new electrical energy started its upward spiral. The years 1895 through 1915 saw rapid changes occur in hydroelectric design and a wide variety of plant styles built. Hydroelectric plant design became fairly well standardized after World War I, with most development in the 1920s and 1930s being related to thermal plants and transmission and distribution.

Hydroelectric Power Helps Build Dams

The Bureau of Reclamation became involved in hydropower production because of its commitment to water resource management in the arid West. The waterfalls of the Reclamation dams make them significant producers of electricity. Hydroelectric power generation has long been an integral part of Reclamation's operations while it is actually a byproduct of water development. In the early days, newly created projects lacked many of the modern conveniences, one of these being electrical power. This made it desirable to take advantage of the potential power source in water.

Powerplants were installed at the dam sites to carry on construction camp activities. Hydropower was put to work lifting, moving, and processing materials to build the dams and dig canals. Powerplants ran sawmills, concrete plants, cableways, giant shovels, and draglines. Night operations were possible because of the lights fed by hydroelectric power. When construction was complete, hydropower drove pumps that provided drainage of conveyed water to lands at higher elevations than could be served by gravity-flow canals.

Surplus power was sold to existing power distribution systems in the area. Local industries, towns and farm consumers benefitted from the low-cost electricity. Much of the construction and operating costs of dams and related facilities were paid for by this sale of surplus power, rather than by the water users alone. This proved to be a great savings to irrigators struggling to survive in the West.

Reclamation's first hydroelectric powerplant was built to aid construction of the Theodore Roosevelt Dam on the Salt River

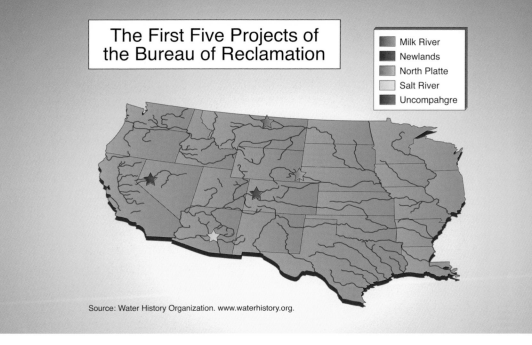

The First Five Projects of the Bureau of Reclamation

- Milk River
- Newlands
- North Platte
- Salt River
- Uncompahgre

Source: Water History Organization. www.waterhistory.org.

about 75 miles northeast of Phoenix, Arizona. Small hydroelectric generators, installed prior to construction, provided energy for construction and for equipment to lift stone blocks into place. Surplus power was sold to the community, and citizens were quick to support expansion of the dam's hydroelectric capacity. A 4,500 kilowatt [kW] powerplant was constructed and, in 1909, five generators were in operation, supplying power for pumping irrigation water and furnishing electricity to the Phoenix area.

Hydroelectric Power and Water Development

Power development, a byproduct of water development, had a tremendous impact on the area's economy and living conditions. Power was sold to farms, cities, and industries. Wells pumped by electricity meant more irrigated land for agriculture, and pumping also lowered water tables in those areas with water logging and alkaline soil problems. By 1916, nine pumping plants were in operation, irrigating more than 10,000 acres. In addition, Reclamation supplied all of the residential and commercial power needs of Phoenix. Cheap hydropower, in abundant supply, attracted industrial development as well. A private company was

The Theodore Roosevelt dam and lake provide large amounts of power for the city of Phoenix.

able to build a large smelter and mill nearby to process low-grade copper ore, using hydroelectric power.

The Theodore Roosevelt Powerplant was one of the first large power facilities constructed by the Federal Government. Its capacity has since been increased from 4,500 kW to over 36,000 kW. . . .

World War I and the Depression

During World War I, Reclamation projects continued to provide water and hydroelectric power to Western farms and ranches. This helped to feed and clothe the Nation, and the power revenues were a welcome source of income to the Federal Government.

The Depression of the 1930s, coupled with widespread floods and drought in the West, spurred the building of great multipurpose Reclamation projects such as Grand Coulee Dam on the Columbia River, Hoover Dam on the lower Colorado River, and the Central Valley Project in California. This was the "big dam" period, and the low-cost hydropower produced by those dams had a profound effect on urban and industrial growth.

The Grand Coulee Dam in Washington state (pictured) was one of several reclamation projects to occur in the wake of the Depression.

Hydroelectricity Powers the War Effort

With the advent of World War II the Nation's need for hydroelectric power soared. At the outbreak of the war, the Axis Nations had three times more available power than the United States. The demand for power was identified in this 1942 statement on "The War Program of the Department of the Interior":

> The war budget of $56 billion will require 154 billion kWh [kilowatt-hours] of electric energy annually for the manufacture of airplanes, tanks, guns, warships, and fighting material, and to equip and serve the men of the Army, Navy and Marine Corps.

Each dollar spent for wartime industry required about 2-3/4 kWh of electric power. The demand exceeded the total production capacity of all existing electric utilities in the United States. To produce enough aluminum to meet the President's goal of 60,000 new planes in 1942 alone required 8.5 billion kWh of electric power.

Hydropower provided one of the best ways for rapidly expanding the country's energy output. Addition of more power-plant units at dams throughout the West made it possible to expand energy production, and construction pushed ahead to speed up the availability of power. In 1941, Reclamation produced more than 5 billion kWh, resulting in a 25 percent increase in aluminum production. By 1944 Reclamation quadrupled its hydroelectric power output.

From 1940 through 1945, Reclamation powerplants produced 47 billion kWh of electricity, enough to make:

- 69,000 airplanes
- 5,000 ships
- 5,000 tanks
- 79,000 machine guns
- 7,000,000 aircraft bombs
- 31,000,000 shells

During the war, Reclamation was the major producer of power in the West where needed resources were located. The supply of low-cost electricity attracted large defense industries to the area. Shipyards, steel mills, chemical companies, oil refineries, and automotive and aircraft factories all needed vast amounts of electrical power. Atomic energy installations were located at Hanford, Washington, to make use of hydropower from Grand Coulee [Dam].

While power output of Reclamation projects energized the war industry, it was also used to process food, light military posts, and meet needs of the civilian population in many areas.

Hydropower in the Postwar Era

With the end of the war, powerplants were put to use in rapidly developing peacetime industries. Hydropower has been vital for the West's industries which use mineral resources or farm products as raw materials. Many industries have depended wholly on Federal hydropower. In fact, periodic low flows on the Columbia River have disrupted manufacturing in that region.

Farming was tremendously important to America during the war and continues to be today. Reclamation delivers 10 trillion gallons of water delivered to more than 31 million people each

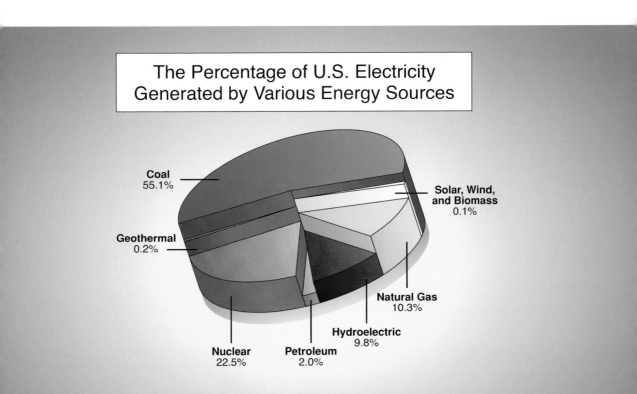

The Percentage of U.S. Electricity Generated by Various Energy Sources

Coal
55.1%

Solar, Wind, and Biomass
0.1%

Geothermal
0.2%

Natural Gas
10.3%

Hydroelectric
9.8%

Nuclear
22.5%

Petroleum
2.0%

Source: Wisconsin Valley Improvement Company, September 2004. www.wvic.com.

year and provides 1 out of 5 Western farmers (140,000) with irrigation water for 10 million farmland acres that produce 60% of the nation's vegetables and 25% of its fruits and nuts.

Hydropower directly benefits rural areas in three ways:

- It produces revenue which contributes toward repayment of irrigation facilities, easing the water user's financial burden.
- It makes irrigation of lands at higher elevations possible through pumping facilities.
- It makes power available for use on the farm for domestic purposes.

Dams built in the U.S. have resulted in a decline in fish populations.

CHAPTER 2

Does Water Power Harm the Environment?

Hydropower Dams Harm the Environment

Elizabeth Grossman

Elizabeth Grossman argues in the following viewpoint that dams have an adverse impact on the environment. Dams alter the natural flow of rivers, causing disruptions in fish migrations. Dams built in the United States have resulted in many once-abundant fish species becoming endangered. Dams also harm the vegetation and wildlife that depend on natural river ecosystems. Grossman contends that none of these harms is justifiable given that dams generate relatively little electricity. In fact, she claims, the majority of dams are built to create lakes for recreational activities. Elizabeth Grossman is a freelance journalist based in Oregon. Her writings include books, articles, essays, and reviews.

Dams and diversions along America's rivers have transformed the country, and in doing so created environmental problems whose resolution will, in many ways, determine how we live in this new century. The vast enterprise of dam building of the past hundred years paralleled the progress of the very American twentieth century. Jobs were created, farms and ranches irrigated and factories built that helped to win world wars and furnish the American dream. Cities rose in the desert, floodplains were drained and rivers channeled to suit civic vision.

Now, barely three generations later, the cost of this extraordinary engineering is acutely apparent. Species of fish once so numerous as to be legendary are now on the brink of extinction. Seasons of destructive flooding, exacerbated by artificially constricted riverbanks, have prompted a reassessment of the value of wetlands as nature's filter, flood-control and reservoir system. . . .

Damage to Fish

Dams alter and block the natural flow of rivers, obstructing fish migration. They change water temperatures and degrade water quality in ways that damage vegetation and wildlife. Dams hold back silt, gravel, debris and nutrients that create a healthy environment for river species. Dams trap sediment and prevent water from reaching the mouths of rivers, disrupting and destroying the

Though they provide valuable power, dams can harm the environment. Dams have depleted snake and salmon populations on this stretch of the Columbia River between Oregon and Washington.

ecology of deltas and estuaries crucial to the development of aquatic species. Many dams, including some of the largest, were built with no fish passage whatsoever. Dams make life especially difficult for anadromous fish, those that are born in the cold water of upland and mountain streams and migrate to the ocean to mature before returning to their native rivers to spawn. Dams have decimated native fish populations and have had a particularly devastating effect on the anadromous fish of the Atlantic and Pacific coasts. On the Colorado River, dams have allowed invasive exotics to thrive, endangering native species. Some dams' reservoirs are now choked with sediment, rendering the dams ineffective and conditions untenable for river species.

Damage to Rivers

When a dam impounds a river, it eliminates the ever changing channels, bends and meanders needed to nurture fish, shellfish and other river species. Dams also disrupt the interaction between a river and its banks, upsetting the habitat of aquatic insects and other organisms on which fish depend for food. Relying on dams for large-scale water storage, and delivering water to places where it does not naturally occur, have long-term effects on the balance between groundwater and surface water and on the quality of the surrounding soil. These ecological costs have economic repercussions. Most large-scale dams built by the government are heavily subsidized, as are the power, irrigation and navigation access they provide. Many end up costing far more than expected, especially when the price of restoration, repair and loss of commercial, tribal and sport fishing is included. And while rarely discussed in this country, large dams may carry another substantial cost, when the land their impoundments flood displaces those who live in the adjacent river valley. Dams, said [Bill] Clinton administration Secretary of the Interior Bruce Babbitt, voicing a significant change in how government officials view dams, "should be judged by the health of the rivers to which they belong."

Dam "Benefits"

Yet we are accustomed to the "benefits" of dams. In the West, cheap, heavily subsidized hydropower, irrigation and shipping

Many dams, such as this one in Massachusetts, are no longer useful. Removing them, however, can cause damage to the environment that has developed around them.

passage directed development of the region's economy. From the earliest days of New England's settlement, local industry grew up around sawmills, gristmills and factories powered by dams. The impoundments and slackwater created by dams are often recreational and residential magnets now ingrained in the custom and character of surrounding communities. Dams for drinking water, flood control and the diversion of wetlands stimulated the growth of urban and agricultural centers.

Removing dams affects all of this. But a great many dams no longer serve the purpose for which they were built, and their small output of hydropower or irrigation water can be provided by other less destructive means.

There are over 75,000 dams on the Army Corps of Engineers' National Inventory of Dams, and that includes only dams over six feet tall. "That means we have been building, on average, one large dam a day, every single day, since the Declaration of Independence," Babbitt said to the Ecological Society of America in 1998. It's estimated that less than 1 percent of the nation's river miles are protected in their natural state, and approximately 600,000 miles of what were free-flowing rivers now lie stagnant behind dams. Virtually no major river in the United States is without a dam. But the nation's dam building peaked in the 1970s, and since 1998, according to the World Commission on Dams, the rate of decommissioning dams in the United States has overtaken the rate of construction.

Small Dams Have Problems Too

When we think about dams, we tend to picture the behemoths of concrete like Grand Coulee and Hoover Dam or the dams of the Tennessee Valley Authority. Most of the dams that block our rivers are far less grandiose. Many are unassuming stretches of mossy cement, masked by a small curtain of falling water. They were built for local enterprises, to water pastures and modest farm fields, to grind grain, turn logs into building boards and sluice small mines. Yet even these smaller dams have seriously detrimental effects on their rivers, especially as many rivers suffer the cumulative effects of multiple dams throughout a watershed. These small dams often become safety hazards as they fall into disrepair and impound deceptively inviting swimming holes.

Controlled Waterways

Dams are so ubiquitous that most of us are utterly unaccustomed to looking at a free-flowing river. It may look like a river, but chances are what you see is a series of impoundments or reservoirs now labeled "lakes." Even the rapids of the Colorado, plunging through the Grand Canyon, apparently the essence of wildness, are subject to flows as tightly controlled as those on a kitchen sink. Because of the controlled flows and the way dams trap sediment, impoundments do not function biologically as a natural lake does. Impoundments develop their own ecology, but it is often at odds with the river's natural ecosystem and can cause trouble for native species. But these "lakes"—whether a small millpond or vast reservoir—often occupy a prominent place in a community. In fact, the stated use or purpose of the

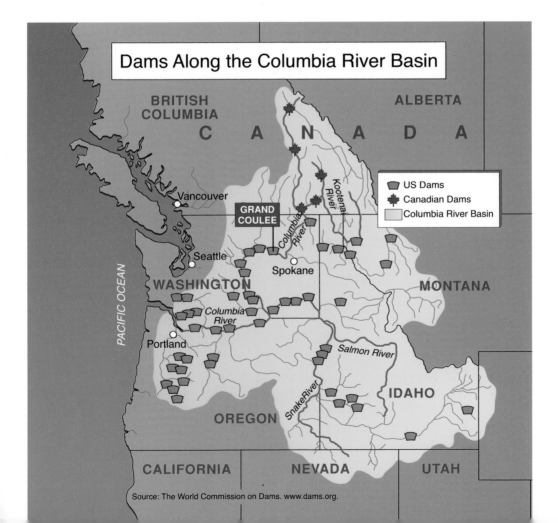

Source: The World Commission on Dams. www.dams.org.

largest number of dams—31.3 percent—in the National Inventory of Dams is recreation.

Although the federal government owns and operates most large hydropower dams in the United States, most of the country's other dams are privately owned. The federal government actually owns only 3 percent of the Inventory's 75,000 dams. Local governments own 17 percent, state governments own 5 percent and public utilities just 2 percent. A large number of these dams—over 1,700, or 15 percent—are of undetermined ownership. Since most state regulations require the state to assume financial responsibility for its abandoned dams, they can easily become a burden to their communities.

Of these 75,000 dams, only 2.9 percent have hydroelectric power as their primary purpose. Only 13.7 percent are primarily devoted to irrigation, less than 10 percent to water supply and 0.3 percent to navigation. Of the inventoried dams, 14.6 percent are used for flood control, 17 percent to store water for farm ponds and fire prevention and 8 percent in mining activity.

Hydropower Dams Contribute to Global Warming

Patrick McCully

Hydropower has long been seen as a clean source of energy since it does not involve the burning of fossil fuels, which produces greenhouse gas emissions. However, in the following selection Patrick McCully disagrees with that assessment. He claims that the flooding created by hydroelectric dams submerges vegetation, causing it to rot. This decaying plant material emits large amounts of methane and carbon dioxide, greenhouse gases that contribute to global warming. According to McCully, the gases emitted by hydropower reservoirs can equal or exceed the amount of greenhouse gases emitted by fossil fuel plants. Patrick McCully is campaigns director for the International Rivers Network, an organization that promotes sound water resources development.

Hydropower's supposed potential for mitigating global warming—because it does not involve fossil-fuel burning—is now seen by the industry as one of its greatest selling points. Five out of 14 speakers at a 1994 international conference on financing dam projects referred to the importance of hydropower as a non-greenhouse gas emitting technology (and none of the speakers referred to hydro as 'cheap'). Also in 1994, state-owned utility Hydro-Québec advertised in energy industry journals that Canadian and US energy utilities 'can help reduce the threat of global warming for all of us' by importing hydroelectricity from Quebec. Some hydro advocates propose that industrialized countries should meet their obligations to limit greenhouse gas emissions under the UN's [United Nations's] framework climate convention by helping to pay for hydrodams in developing countries.

Hydropower Is Not 'Climate-Friendly'

Global warming is clearly a very real and massive threat to human society and the natural world, and technologies and modes of political and social organisation which can minimize greenhouse gas emissions—while not exacerbating other environmental and social problems—need urgently to be brought into use. Hydropower, however, is not only socially and environmentally destructive, but is also far from being as 'climate-friendly' as its proponents allege. While little research has yet been done on greenhouse gas emissions from reservoirs, what has been carried out suggests that hydropower reservoirs, espe-

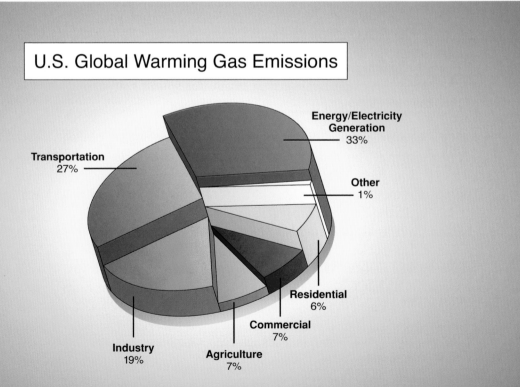

U.S. Global Warming Gas Emissions

Energy/Electricity Generation 33%

Transportation 27%

Other 1%

Residential 6%

Commercial 7%

Agriculture 7%

Industry 19%

Source: U.S. Environmental Protection Agency, 2002. www.greenmachinestour.org.

cially those in tropical forest areas, can make a significant contribution to global warming, in some cases as much or even more than fossil fuel-burning power plants producing an equivalent amount of electricity.

How Plants and Forests Balance Greenhouse Gases

Through the processes of growth and decay, soils, forests and wetlands continuously consume and emit large amounts of carbon dioxide (CO_2) and methane (CH_4), the two most important non-synthetic greenhouse gases. For mature forests and grasslands, the consumption and emission of CO_2 is usually in balance, and the ecosystems act as huge carbon stores with—as long as they remain undisturbed—no net effect on the concentration of greenhouse gases in the atmosphere. Many soils, however, consume more methane than they emit and are therefore net methane sinks. Temperate peatlands are sinks of both CO_2 and CH_4; tropical wetlands, on the other hand, are major sources of methane. Natural lakes are usually sources of methane but often sinks for carbon dioxide. Just as the fluxes of these gases from different ecosystems to and from the atmosphere vary widely, so does the amount of the carbon stored in biomass and soils: natural forests, for example, can store 20 to 100 times as much carbon per unit area as farmlands. The biomass of tropical forests tends to contain far more carbon than temperate forests; temperate grassland soils, on the other hand, can contain more carbon that tropical forest vegetation and soils put together.

When these ecosystems are flooded, the pattern of the fluxes of CO_2 and CH_4 with the atmosphere is totally altered. Peat, which as a living ecosystem consumed the gases, when flooded rots and is a net source of them. Plants and soils decompose when flooded and will eventually release almost all of their stored carbon. Permanently flooding tropical wetlands will tend to increase their methane emissions and make them a net source of CO_2. Gases produced by reservoirs can be emitted through continuous diffusion into the atmosphere from the surface of the water; in sudden pulses when deep water in the reservoir rises to the surface in cold weather (cooling the water

When flooded by dams, peat bogs can overproduce greenhouse gases such as carbon dioxide. These peat bogs are located near a lake in France.

at the surface makes it denser and so causes it to sink); and from deep water being discharged through turbines.

The Fearnside Greenhouse Gas Study

The most comprehensive study of reservoir greenhouse gas emissions has been done by Philip Fearnside of the Brazilian National Institute for Research in Amazonia (INPA). Fearnside calculated the impact on global warming of Balbina and Tucuruí dams [in Brazil] over the first 50 years of their lives by assessing the amount of forest they flooded and the rate at which vegetation would decay at different depths of their reservoirs. He concluded that immediately after reservoir filling there is a huge pulse of CO_2 emissions, which then steadily decline over the years. Around half of the total CO_2 emissions from Balbina happened within seven years of impoundment, almost all of the gas being released from the parts of decaying trees above the water line.

The warm, nutrient-rich and severely oxygen-depleted water at the bottom of these shallow reservoirs creates ideal conditions for the methane-producing bacteria which feed on decaying vegetation. The rate of decay in the deoxygenated bottom layer of a tropical reservoir is incredibly slow—even leaves can take centuries to completely decompose. Methane production is only partly related to the original amount of flooded biomass as it is also emitted by the decay of aquatic plants and of organic matter which the river carries into the reservoir. For these reasons, methane emissions are fairly constant over time and do not decline significantly as the reservoir matures.

This area of Brazilian rain forest was destroyed after water from a dam created the Tucuruí Reservoir.

Reservoirs Emit More Greenhouse Gases

Fearnside calculates that in 1990 (six years after Tucuruí started to fill and three years after the gates were closed at Balbina) Tucuruí Reservoir emitted 9,450,000 tonnes of carbon dioxide and 90,000 tonnes of methane; Balbina emitted 23,750,000 tonnes of carbon dioxide and 140,000 tonnes of methane. Combining the effects of the two gases, Fearnside estimated that Tucuruí had 60 per cent as much impact on global warming as a coal-fired plant generating the same amount of electricity—but 50 per cent more impact than a gas-fired power station. Balbina Reservoir, meanwhile, had *26 times more* impact on global warming than the emissions from an equivalent coal-fired power station. While the emissions from the reservoirs will slowly decline over the years as the flooded biomass decays, the global warming impact of Balbina will always be far higher than that from equivalent fossil fuel generation.

Fearnside's paper follows a study by a team of researchers led by John Rudd of the Canadian government's Freshwater Institute which estimated that there are also substantial emissions of CO_2 and methane from reservoirs in northern Canada. Rudd and his co-workers measured per-hectare gas releases from flooded forests and bogs and then extrapolated these findings to estimate the average annual emissions over 50 years of two large hydroelectric reservoirs in northern Manitoba. The researchers concluded that the contribution to global warming for every kilowatt-hour generated at Grand Rapids Dam was around the same as that from a gas-fired plant, while a kilowatt-hour from the huge Churchill/Nelson hydro scheme contributed only around an eighth as much as a gas plant.

Hydropower Dams Can Reduce Global Warming

Alain Tremblay, Louis Varfalvy, Charlotte Roehm, and Michelle Garneau

In the following selection Alain Tremblay, Louis Varfalvy, Charlotte Roehm, and Michelle Garneau argue that hydropower is one of the cleanest ways to generate electricity. Using new measuring techniques they developed, the team studied greenhouse gas emissions at several hydroelectric reservoirs throughout the world. They claim that reservoirs in northern climates emit far fewer greenhouse gases—gases created by rotting vegetation within the reservoir—than do fossil fuel plants. The researchers also discovered that some reservoirs in tropical regions emit more gases than those in temperate areas. Still, Tremblay and his collegues conclude, taken together, hydroelectric reservoirs emit far fewer greenhouse gas emissions than do fossil fuel plants. Tremblay and Varfalvy are scientists at Hydro-Quebec Production in Canada, and Roehm and Garneau teach at the University of Quebec in Montreal, Canada.

The major greenhouse gases [GHGs] are carbon dioxide (CO_2), methane (CH_4) and nitrous oxide (N_2O). These gases are emitted from both natural aquatic (lakes, rivers, estuaries, wetlands) and terrestrial ecosystems (forest, soils) as well

Alain Tremblay, Louis Varfalvy, Charlotte Roehm, and Michelle Garneau, "The Issue of Greenhouse Gases from Hydroelectric Reservoirs: From Boreal to Tropical Regions," background paper delivered to United Nations symposium on hydropower and sustainable development, in Beijing, October 27-29, 2004. Reproduced by permission of the authors.

Some believe that wetlands formed by dams, such as these at the foot of Mt. Bachelor in Oregon, can reduce greenhouse gas emissions.

as from anthropogenic man made sources. According to both the European Environment Agency and the United States Environmental Protection Agency, CO_2 emissions account for the largest share of GHGs. . . . Fossil fuel combustion for transportation and electricity generation are the main source of CO_2, contributing to more than 50% of the emissions. Thermal power plants [those running on fossil fuels] represent 66% of the world's electric generation capacity. Hydropower represents about 20% of the world's electricity generation capacity and emits 35 to 70 times less GHGs per TWh [terawatt-hour] than thermal power plants. Nevertheless, for the last few years GHG emissions from freshwater reservoirs and their contribution to the increase of GHGs in the atmosphere are actually at the heart of a worldwide debate concerning the electricity generating sector. However, to our knowledge, there are few emission measurements available from these environments although they are at the heart of the debate concerning methods of energy production.

Devising a Better Way to Measure GHGs

In this context, Hydro-Québec and its partners have adapted a technique to measure gross GHG emissions. . . . These measurements were done in order to compare the results with those obtained by other methods, and to better assess the gross emissions of GHG from aquatic ecosystems in boreal (northern climate), semi-arid and tropical regions. This was done also to adequately estimate the contribution of reservoirs compared to natural water bodies in these regions, as well as to compare properly various options of electricity generation. . . .

The Results of the Study

The results [of our study using the new measuring technique] come from a sampling program that was conducted since 2001 in many boreal Canadian provinces, in the semi-arid western region of the United States of America and in tropical regions of Panama and French Guiana. The results and conclusions also benefit from Alain Tremblay's Synthesis "Greenhouse Gas Emissions: Fluxes and Processes, Hydroelectric Reservoirs and Natural Environments". One must keep in mind, that most of the data on GHG from hydroelectric reservoirs come from research and measurements in boreal regions and, to a lesser extent, from a follow-up environmental program of Petit Saut reservoir in tropical French Guiana and a few Brazilian reservoirs.

The . . . processes determining the fate of carbon in reservoirs are similar to those occurring in natural aquatic ecosystems.

> **ANOTHER OPINION**
>
> ### Hydro Electric Dams and Global Warming
>
> "Even if some hydroelectric dams turn out to be net producers of greenhouse gases, we can't assume that all hydroelectric dams cause more in warming effects from methane production than they prevent in avoided carbon dioxide release."
>
> Randall Parker, "Do Hydroelectric Dams Cause Global Warming?" February 28, 2005. www.futurepundit.com.

However, some of these processes might be temporally modified in reservoirs due to the flooding of terrestrial ecosystems which results from the creation of reservoirs. In boreal reservoirs, environmental follow-up programs have clearly shown that these changes generally last less than 10 years. However in tropical reservoirs, these changes can extend over a longer period of time according to the conditions of impoundment.

In the case of reservoirs, it is known that the amount of GHGs emitted at the air-water interface varies over time. In fact, there is an initial peak which occurs immediately after impoundment. . . . The increase of GHG emissions in reservoirs shortly after flooding is related to the release of nutrients, enhanced bacterial activity and decomposition of labile carbon. Magnitude of emissions for both reservoirs and natural aquatic

While dam-formed reservoirs such as the Vigario Reservoir in Brazil (pictured) emit greenhouse gases, they tend to do so at much lower levels than other power-generating methods.

systems depend on physico-chemical characteristics of the water body and on the incoming carbon from the watershed. . . .

The Advantages of Hydroelectricity

There is a convergence in the results, from both boreal and tropical reservoirs, that clearly illustrates that reservoirs do emit GHGs for a period of about 10–15 years. Therefore, according to the GHG emission factors reported for hydro reservoirs both by IAEA and by various studies performed during the last decade on a variety and a great number of reservoirs, it can be concluded that the energy produced with the force of water is very efficient, showing emission factors between one and two orders of magnitude lower than the thermal alternatives. However, in some cases, tropical reservoirs, such as the Petit Saut reservoir in French Guiana or some Brazilian reservoirs, GHG emissions could, during a certain time period, significantly exceed emissions from thermal alternatives. . . . With respect to GHG emissions from hydropower . . . , we can provide the following general observations:

- GHG emission factors from hydroelectricity generated in boreal regions are significantly smaller than corresponding emission factors from thermal power plants alternatives; . . .

- GHG emission factors from hydroelectricity generated in tropical regions cover a much wider range of values. . . . Based on a 100 year lifetime, these emissions factors could either reach very low or very high values, varying from less than 1% to more than 200% of the emission factors reported for thermal power plant generation;

- Net GHG emission factors for hydro power, should be at first sight 30% to 50% lower than the emission factors currently reported.

The vast majority of hydroelectric reservoirs built in boreal regions are emitting very small amounts of GHGs, and represent therefore one of the cleanest ways to generate electricity. In some tropical reservoirs, anoxic conditions could lead to larger emissions. Therefore, GHG emissions from tropical reservoirs should be considered on a case by case base level.

4 ⮞ Glen Canyon Dam Is Harmful and Unnecessary

Christopher Peterson

Controversy over Glen Canyon Dam and its reservoir, Lake Powell, has been raging for years. The dam was originally built to help the arid Southwest manage its water resources and to supply electricity to western cities. However, environmentalists, archeologists, and anthropologists claim that the dam has flooded ancient Indian sites and destroyed the river ecosystem. The debate over Glen Canyon Dam is representative of arguments waged all over the world concerning the use of dams.

In the following selection Christopher Peterson argues that the dam does not produce enough hydroelectric power to justify keeping it. He contends that both the dam and the reservoir have negatively impacted the river system and the surrounding environment. Peterson concludes, therefore, that the lake should be drained. Christopher Peterson is the executive director of the Glen Canyon Institute, an organization working to restore Glen Canyon.

In 1963, Glen Canyon, the wild heart of the Colorado Plateau, was flooded by Lake Powell for water storage. Backing up the surplus waters of the Colorado River nearly 200 miles, Glen Canyon Dam created 200-mile-long Lake Powell, which generates a small amount of electricity, and provides a water skiing destination in the middle of the desert. Legendary

Glen Canyon's 125 major side canyons were lost when the dam was constructed, and the Grand Canyon and Glen Canyon ecosystems have been badly damaged due to the dam.

The Era of Water Surplus Is Over

Today, the water surplus at Lake Powell, accumulated over the past half-century, is nearly gone. When the dam was built, demand was far less, but today's demand for water across the basin exceeds the supply of water available from the Colorado River. Demand is predicted to continue to grow, leaving no extra water to store at Lake Powell in the future. Instead, water shortages and transfers from agriculture to urban use will prevail, with captured flood waters immediately distributed to thirsty cities. Lake Powell was a "one trick pony" whose usefulness has expired.

Growing Demand for Western Water Is Draining Lake Powell

Despite premature reports that the drought is over and reservoirs across the West may again be full soon, it is crucial to recognize that growing water demand is draining Lake Powell; the drought has only highlighted the issue. Lake Powell will rise

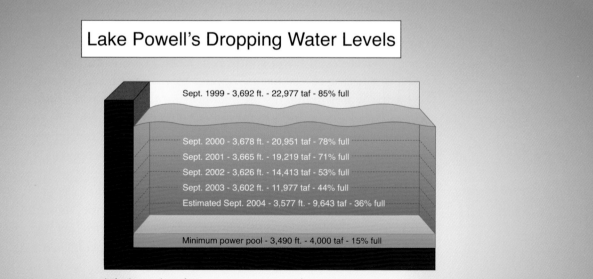

Lake Powell's Dropping Water Levels

Sept. 1999 - 3,692 ft. - 22,977 taf - 85% full

Sept. 2000 - 3,678 ft. - 20,951 taf - 78% full
Sept. 2001 - 3,665 ft. - 19,219 taf - 71% full
Sept. 2002 - 3,626 ft. - 14,413 taf - 53% full
Sept. 2003 - 3,602 ft. - 11,977 taf - 44% full
Estimated Sept. 2004 - 3,577 ft. - 9,643 taf - 36% full

Minimum power pool - 3,490 ft. - 4,000 taf - 15% full

*taf = thousand acre feet

Source: Closed Circuit Newsletter, May 28, 2004. www.wapa.gov.

and fall in the coming years as political maneuvering for valuable water . . . builds. Occasional water surpluses at Lake Powell will be quickly withdrawn for thirsty cities both up and downstream from Glen Canyon. Also, the depletion and recharge processes will be compounded by the effects of on-going climate change in the West.

Lake Powell Wastes Water

Powell reservoir loses on average 800,000 acre-feet of water annually to evaporation and bank seepage. This is three times the state of Nevada's Colorado River allocation and enough to supply the city of Los Angeles for at least a year. Water managers throughout the West are taking steps toward moving the remaining Colorado River surplus water to other storage facilities in underground aquifers, headwater and offstream reservoirs, and to Lake Mead.

Lake Mead Is Enough

Lake Powell will never be kept full again. Recent studies on the future hydrology of the Colorado River demonstrate that Lake Powell will be below its current 35% of full most of the next century. Lake Mead, alone, is adequate for seasonal water storage. The occasional flood captures at Lake Powell can easily be stored in existing reservoir and aquifer facilities elsewhere across the basin. Water managers are recognizing the need and opportunities developing, and are taking steps to ensure their own respective water rights are protected. Those steps will render the water storage purpose of Lake Powell unnecessary and obsolete.

America's Lost National Park

Glen Canyon is legendary for its cultural significance, as well as for unparalleled beauty, with lush waterfalls, stone arches, soaring mesas, twisting narrows, hoodoos, natural bridges, ancient ruins, and rock art. Glen Canyon's splendor has been lost

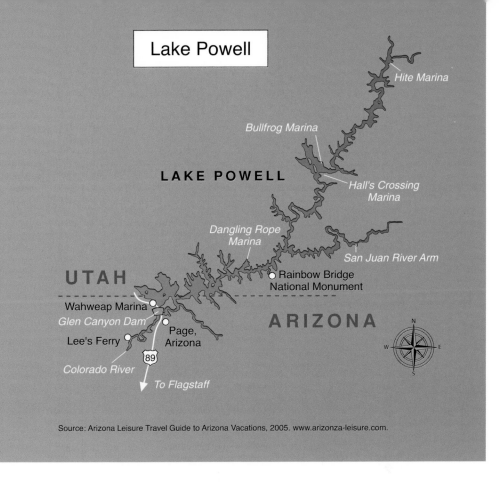

Source: Arizona Leisure Travel Guide to Arizona Vacations, 2005. www.arizonza-leisure.com.

for forty years, but now this spectacular lost canyon wonderland is found and has triggered significant international attention. People around the world are clamoring to witness a free flowing Colorado River breathing new life into places like Cathedral in the Desert, with ancient ruins and priceless historical sites emerging from the depths of Lake Powell. The importance of protecting these precious resources is essential in light of increased visitation to the emerging landscape.

Right now, hundreds of spectacular features in Glen Canyon landscape have reemerged and the canyon is naturally restoring itself. More than 40 miles of both the Colorado and San Juan Rivers, and hundreds of miles of side-canyons are rapidly recovering. The biological heart of the Colorado River is proving remarkably resilient as vegetation, native fish, birds and the entire spectrum of desert wildlife species are reclaiming the revealed [canyon]. . . .

The growing number of visitors to these fragile restoring canyons presents a significant management challenge to the National Parks Service in Glen Canyon as the agency adapts to the management challenges presented by the changing user impacts. Precious cultural, historical, and biological resources must be protected against visitor impacts. As visitor use shifts within Glen Canyon, "America's Lost National Park" should be managed as the keystone of the Grand Circle of National Parks across the rugged Colorado Plateau from Grand Canyon to Mesa Verde and Capitol Reef to Rainbow Bridge.

The Glen Canyon Dam was constructed in 1963, and has been a source of controversy ever since.

Restoring Glen Canyon Will Save Grand Canyon

The environmental impacts on Grand Canyon caused by Glen Canyon Dam are undeniable. The failing health of the fragile Grand Canyon ecosystem are well documented by the Federal Government and the tribes. Endangered Species populations in the Grand Canyon continue to drop while nutrient-rich sediment deposits grow rapidly behind Glen Canyon Dam at the rate of 30,000 dump-truck loads daily. . . .

Glen Canyon Institute is currently working to ensure the emerging resources within Glen Canyon are protected and documented. Right now, reservoir levels are projected to temporarily rise 40+ feet, once again drowning incredible features such as legendary Cathedral in the Desert, Fort Moqui, and Gregory Natural Bridge. They will be under water for a few months until the water levels recede again in early fall [2004]. This extra water could easily be stored in half-empty Lake Mead.

In the short term, surplus water should be stored in Lake Mead, where there is ample capacity. Open the gates, let the river flow through Glen Canyon.

Glen Canyon Dam Is Necessary

5

Paul Ostapuk

Controversy over Glen Canyon Dam and its reservoir, Lake Powell, is ongoing. Critics say the dam has damaged the river ecosystem while supporters claim the dam is needed to help western states manage their water resources and to generate electricity for western cities. In the following article Paul Ostapuk contends that Lake Powell is essential to the American Southwest. The lake, he says, holds water in times of drought, enabling those living in western states to survive dry years. Ostapuk also claims that the dam pays for itself by selling desperately needed electricity to growing western cities. Paul Ostapuk is a member of the board of directors for Friends of Lake Powell.

Shafts of filtered light pour across the dry Colorado Plateau, as a lone boat on Lake Powell makes a slow, graceful arc and heads toward Antelope Point Marina on the Navajo Reservation. Spring runoff has been good, and the lake is up 50 feet, reversing a five-year downward trend during extreme drought conditions.

The drought prompted rumors of the lake's demise, but looking across Lake Powell, I struggle to comprehend its immensity—465 feet deep at the dam, with 12 million acre-feet of water in storage and extending 160 miles uplake from Page.

Paul Ostapuk, "Guest Opinion: Thank Heaven We Have Lakes Powell, Mead," *Tuscon Citizen*, September 8, 2005. Reproduced by permission of the author.

The Dam Benefits Western States

Drought and water-level fluctuations are nothing new for Lake Powell. A five-year drought in the 1990s drew the lake down to within 10 feet of today's level. Three years later, Lake Powell was essentially full. Such is the ebb and flow of the Colorado River.

Lakes Mead and Powell are the big canteens for the Colorado River system. They hedge the seven Colorado River states and their growing populations from the specter of drought. "If we didn't have Lake Powell in place before we started this drought, Lake Mead would be virtually empty at this point," says Tom Ryan, Bureau of Reclamation hydrologist. "A lot of people would be in a world of hurt."

Lake Powell has broad political support in both Colorado River basins. Although technically built for the Upper Basin, the Arizona Legislature passed a resolution years ago, urging Congress and the president to oppose any effort to breach Glen Canyon Dam. The Navajo Nation said "removing Lake Powell

Supporters of dams on the Colorado River, such as the Glen Canyon and Hoover dams, say that water fluctuations that cause "bathtub rings" are part of the natural ebb and flow of the river.

would wreak disaster on the economic and social welfare of the Navajo Nation." The Hopi said they "do not believe that removing Glen Canyon Dam . . . is a viable or realistic option."

Dams Pay for Themselves with Hydroelectric Power

How valuable are dams on the Colorado River? Besides providing drinking water, drought protection and recreation, big dams pay for themselves by using the free fall of water to spin turbines and create clean hydroelectric power.

At Glen Canyon Dam, this means nearly $90 million of annual net revenue for the federal government and a source of low-cost power to nearly 150 nonprofit energy distributors in the West. When you factor in all the economic spin-offs, no wonder economists calculate that large river systems with dams are 25 times more economically productive than rivers without them.

Critics of the Dam Are Wrong

The Colorado River system has a full spectrum of dams, federal wilderness areas and national parks, monuments and recreation areas. We raft and hike; we drink; we irrigate crops.

Groups such as the Glen Canyon Institute, whose mission is to drain Lake Powell, offer a different reality. Their vision is one of removing water infrastructures and preventing reservoirs from refilling once droughts deplete them. To quote Wade Graham, an institute trustee, in reference to Lake Powell's low level: "Drought didn't drain the reservoir . . . it was the rising demand for water."

We can't blame the Upper Basin. Its annual water use increased only from 4 million to 4.4 million acre-feet during the drought. We can't blame the Lower Basin, either. California actually reduced its annual intake of Colorado River water, to 4.4 million from 5.2 million acre-feet.

The real culprit is the extreme nature of drought and a slow reluctance by federal managers to instigate shortage criteria. Thank heaven we had water stored in Lakes Powell and Mead!

Now normal conditions have returned, and Lake Powell has risen 50 feet. The Bureau of Reclamation predicts a further upward trend through 2006. Lake Powell is doing exactly what it

The water from Lake Mead is used for drinking, power, irrigation, and recreation.

was designed to do. The severity of the drought has, however, drawn the attention of federal water managers. The Bureau of Reclamation has opened a public process to develop low-water management strategies for Lakes Powell and Mead.

Evaporation Is Not an Issue

The Glen Canyon Institute denies that a Lake Powell comeback is possible. It claims the lake's initial filling was a fluke produced by unlikely back-to-back 100-year floods in the mid-1980s. The truth is, Lake Powell filled slowly during drought and reached full pool in 1980—well before the big floods of 1983 and 1984.

Bemoaning the 3 percent annual evaporation rate on Lake Powell, environmental groups neglect to mention that moving water to hotter, lower elevations increases the evaporative rate. Lake Mead evaporates at a rate of 5 percent. In Tempe Town Lake, evaporation increases to nearly 40 percent. Should we drain these lakes to save water? Of course not.

Lakes Mead and Powell Are Necessary

Lake Mead provides water for drinking, power, recreation and irrigation of a million acres of farmland. Tempe has seen millions of dollars of development around its new lakefront property. Water in an arid landscape is a magnet that returns many times over the initial investment.

In the West, great investments were made to build our water infrastructures. Proposals to remove them have no base of political support and are merely sideshows to the real issues of water management and population growth.

Drought conditions on the Colorado River will come and go, but Lake Powell is here to stay. It now stores 4 trillion gallons of water. Out West, droughts are never really "over." Water managers store water during wet years and carefully manage water to survive dry years ahead. That is why water storage projects are so very important in the West.

And that is why we have Lake Powell.

CHAPTER 3

Can Water Power Meet Future Energy Needs?

Hydroelectric turbine generators like these account for up to ten percent of the United States electricity production.

Strict Regulations Can Help Make Hydropower More Attractive

Foundation for Water and Energy Education

In the following selection the Foundation for Water and Energy Education (FWEE) claims that hydropower supplies more than 80 percent of Northwestern states' energy needs. To make sure that these states continue to reap the benefits of this renewable energy source, the association asserts that the adverse environmental impacts of dams will have to be addressed. FWEE says that numerous federal and state agencies are working to make hydroelectric plants less harmful to the environment, which will help guarantee a positive future for hydropower. The Foundation for Water and Energy Education provides information on the use of water and hydropower in the Northwestern United States.

About 20% of the world's electricity is generated by using hydropower. In the United States, this resource accounts for up to 10% of the nation's supply of electricity. This 10% can be thought of in the following ways:

- Hydropower produces more than 90,000 megawatts of electricity annually, which is enough to meet the needs of 28.3 million consumers.

- Hydropower accounts for over 90% of all electricity that comes from renewable resources (e.g., solar, geothermal, wind, biomass).
- Hydropower is generated at only 3% of the nation's 80,000 dams.

In the Northwest, hydropower is an even larger part of each person's daily life. Up to 80% of the electricity in the Northwest is produced by hydropower each year. That's enough electricity to meet the needs of 13.6 million homes. And because hydropower is one of the lowest cost forms of energy, most Northwest residents have a significantly lower electric bill than residents in other parts of the country.

The History of Hydropower

Rivers, lakes and streams are nature's way of collecting water from the hydrologic cycle and carrying it back to the ocean for

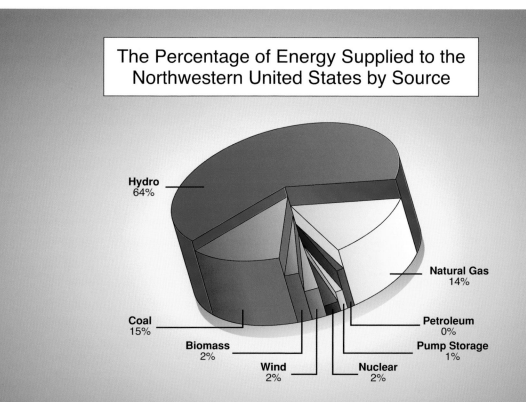

The Percentage of Energy Supplied to the Northwestern United States by Source

Hydro 64%

Natural Gas 14%

Coal 15%

Petroleum 0%

Biomass 2%

Pump Storage 1%

Wind 2%

Nuclear 2%

Source: Northwest Power and Conservation Council, "How Much Northwest Energy Comes from Hydropower?" April 4, 2005. www.nwcouncil.org.

Hydropower provides water for the irrigation of crops. Here, circular irrigated crop fields line the Columbia River on the Oregon-Washington border.

the cycle to begin again. Plants and animals depend on both this cycle and the rivers for survival. As human interaction with rivers increases, maintaining a balance with the plants and wildlife that also depend on the river system becomes more complex and diverse.

Throughout history, people have hunted and fished along rivers. For centuries, rivers have been used to irrigate land for crops. And for generations, paddle wheels used hydropower to harness the force of falling water. With the advent of hydropower, man could operate mills for such things as grinding grain and cutting timber. In harmony with the current, rivers also serve as arteries for passage of fish beneath the surface and all manner of boats above the surface. All of these interactions and shifting balances began before the advent of hydroelectric power production.

Hydropower Helps Develop the Northwest

Hydropower came of age at the turn of the century when many technological advances were being put in place to further tap the ability of the hydrologic cycle and rivers to help meet the needs of society. Technology became available to build larger dams that could better control flooding and irrigate more land. For instance the Grand Coulee Dam, which has the capacity to generate more electricity than any other dam in North America, was built with the primary purpose of turning the Northwest into another bread basket for the nation. Along with other irrigation projects, six percent of the Columbia River Basin's yearly runoff is now diverted to irrigate about 7.6 million acres of land annually. And with the development of locks and other technologies larger and larger cargo vessels were able to navigate rivers. In the Northwest, the result is that each year about 17 million tons of cargo are carried along the Columbia and Snake rivers from the Pacific Ocean.

Water Powers the Northwest

Using hydropower to generate electricity is part of this technological leap. The best known hydroelectric projects are associated with the large dams that have large reservoirs which generate thousands of megawatts of electricity on demand. In fact, the six largest dams in Oregon, Washington and Idaho account for 50% of available hydroelectric power in these states.

For the Northwest as a whole, there are about 160 hydroelectric projects. For the projects which use reservoirs, there are also new recreational opportunities that many people have come to enjoy. Many hydroelectric projects, however, do not use a reservoir. These are called "run-of-river" projects because they do not store significant amounts of water. Instead, they rely on the normal river flow.

Previous generations successfully harnessed this renewable resource in a manner that has developed a standard of living in a way few would consider giving up. Using rivers to meet so many needs, however, also results in significant environmental and cultural impacts. Addressing these impacts and maintaining a balance with the plants, fish and wildlife that also depend on the river has never been more difficult. This and future generations are being asked to meet this challenge.

Hydropower and the Environmental Balance

As mentioned, dams that are part of a hydroelectric project also help control flooding. And by using this renewable resource, up to 249 tons of carbon dioxide are not released into the earth's atmosphere each year since fossil fuels like oil and coal are not burned to generate electricity. Because the release of carbon dioxide contributes to environmental concerns related to ozone depletion and global warming, hydropower represents an important environmental benefit in this regard.

Hydroelectric projects, like any energy resource, do have environmental impacts. In the Northwest, the most serious concerns often relate to fish passage. The 1992 listing of sockeye salmon and three other stocks of chinook salmon (spring, summer and fall) as endangered species intensified historic and continuing debates over restoring fish runs. Releasing water to speed up downstream fish migration has been one of many measures taken to preserve fish runs. In 1994, for instance, nearly 11 million acre feet of water was made available to help juvenile salmon and steelhead migrate downstream.

Research Helps Mitigate Concerns

Measures such as water releases, however, are being taken within the context of scientific inquiry and research that is the subject of much debate. For these reasons, the hydro industry and others continue to explore and implement several mitigation strategies that address hatchery, habitat, harvesting, and hydro operation practices. Examples of such strategies include fish screens, surface collection and bypass systems, fish ladders, strobe lights, the catching of squawfish that prey on juvenile salmon, and new turbine designs. In fact, since the 1980s over two billion dollars has been spent on salmon recovery measures by Northwest ratepayers. As these efforts continue, scientific inquiry and research findings will continue to play a central role in guiding efforts.

The hydroelectric industry, however, cannot address environmental issues, e.g., fish migration or preserving wildlife

The ways that hydropower affects river life, such as these sockeye salmon that run in the Cedar River in Washington, is actively researched.

habitats, in isolation from other industries and individuals that use the rivers. Every action and every user of a river is part of the overall balance. As a result, any search for balance that considers the Northwest's interests as a whole also needs to calculate and mitigate the effects of multiple impacts. Examples include irrigation, timber, mining and the building of homes and industries near the river system. In the case of salmon, for instance, ocean fishing that captures salmon returning to the river system is part of the overall balance.

Federal Regulations Are Important

Most hydroelectric projects across the United States are licensed by the Federal Energy Regulatory Commission (FERC). Many of these licenses, which are required to operate a hydroelectric project, are coming up for renewal during the next ten years. A central piece of receiving a new license is to examine environmental impacts and include the public in both reviewing and considering mitigation and enhancement strategies regarding these impacts. For anyone interested in the river system, becoming informed and heard in these debates is vitally important.

The process for being heard, however, extends well beyond engaging with those who generate hydropower and FERC. Numerous federal and state agencies can become involved in the process. Examples include the National Marine Fisheries Service, U.S. Fish and Wildlife Service, National Parks Service, the Environmental Protection Agency, state fish and wildlife agencies, state water resource agencies and the state agency with Clean Water Act authority. Beyond this crisscrossing of government authority are many tribal governments and non-profit groups with significant interests and concerns. Examples of non-profit groups include American Rivers, the Sierra Club, Trout Unlimited, fishing and hunting associations, and boating groups.

With so many interests participating, and because the issues being addressed are often quite complex, the relicensing process often takes between five to ten years to complete. Regardless of length, becoming an early and informed participant is of benefit to all.

Small Hydropower Projects Can Benefit Rural Communities

Patrick McCully

Small hydropower projects can benefit rural and poor communities, according to Patrick McCully in the following selection. While not able to generate the massive amounts of power produced by giant hydropower facilities, hydro projects on a smaller scale can generate enough power to meet the needs of small communities. These facilities can often be built with local materials and labor, making them more affordable than large dams. Patrick McCully is campaigns director for the International Rivers Network, an organization working to promote sound water resources development.

Small hydro cannot be seen as a direct 'alternative' to the power from large hydro on a worldwide scale, although in some cases a number of small-hydro schemes may be an appropriate alternative to a single large dam. Small-hydro plants have by definition a relatively low power output, and cumulatively they can never provide more than a very small proportion of global electricity supply. Small hydro, however, is well suited to rural areas of poor countries and remote settlements in industrialized countries where electricity demand is relatively low and the costs for connecting villages to national distribution systems high (and also of course where there are fast-flowing, perennial rivers and streams).

Small Hydro History

The generation of electricity from small-hydro plants dates back to the 1880s. Over the following half century, many thousands of small-hydro turbines were installed in Europe and North America. By the 1930s, however, many of these plants began to be abandoned, mainly because of the subsidized growth of electricity distribution grids fed from fossil fuel and large hydro plants, which provided a better quality of electricity, less prone to fluctuations in voltage and frequency. The long decline of small hydro began to be reversed in the 1970s with technological advances which largely solved the problems of fluctuating output, and various forms of government subsidies. Small hydro has also been boosted in many countries by regulatory changes which encourage independent power producers to sell electricity to the big power generation and distribution utilities.

Small Hydro Defined

There is no consistent definition for what constitutes 'small' hydro. Most industry publications and organizations describe small hydro as a plant with up to 10 MW [megawatt] installed capacity, with sub-categories of mini-hydro (below 1MW), micro-hydro (below 100 kW [kilowatt]) and, occasionally, pico-hydro (below 20 kW). Individual countries, however, have widely differing definitions: China defines mini-hydro as up to 500 kW, and small as up to 25 MW; small hydro in Japan is up to 50 MW; in Sweden the upper limit for small hydro is only 1.5 MW. Micro-hydro plants need not produce electrical power: in many rural areas micro-hydro is still used to generate mechanical power for food processing—grinding grains, hulling rice, extracting edible oil—or for small industrial units such as saw mills and cotton gins.

The Many Forms of Small Hydro

Small-hydro stations come in many different forms. Those towards the upper limit of the definition tend to be scaled-down versions of large hydro plants, impounding water behind a concrete, earth or rock dam. Micro plants, however, rarely need a dam, but instead divert part of the river behind a small weir

Small-hydro stations, such as this one in Cambodia, are able to generate enough power to sustain small communities without harming the environment.

which keeps the water at the intake at a constant depth. Micro-hydro plants exploit the high 'head' (the vertical distance which water fails) available on mountain streams by diverting water into a channel which follows the contour of the hillside, then down a steeply sloping penstock pipe into a powerhouse, and then finally through a short tailrace back into the river, often a considerable distance downstream of the weir. In flatter areas where the lack of head is compensated by greater flows, the diverted water flows almost straight from the weir into the powerhouse, then back into the river.

Canadian government researchers calculate that in 1992 the worldwide installed capacity of small hydro (unless otherwise stated the term is used here to mean less than 10 MW) was 19,500 MW—3 per cent of total installed hydro capacity. Nearly two-fifths of small-hydro capacity is in Western Europe and just over one-fifth in North America. The Canadian researchers give an 'optimistic' projection that, with modest government support for small hydro, worldwide installed capacity could almost quadruple by the year 2020. Realistically, however, objections to the larger small-hydro plants on environmental and social grounds mean that the worldwide growth of small hydro will probably be much smaller.

The Advantages of Small Hydro

A major advantage of micro- and mini-hydro for less industrialized countries is that most, and often all, of its components can be built with local or regional expertise, materials and capital. Nepal, Peru, India, Costa Rica, Chile, Brazil and especially China each have numerous indigenous companies producing mini-hydro turbines. The low cost and decentralized nature of mini-hydro plants mean that they can be community owned, even in very poor regions, with any profits

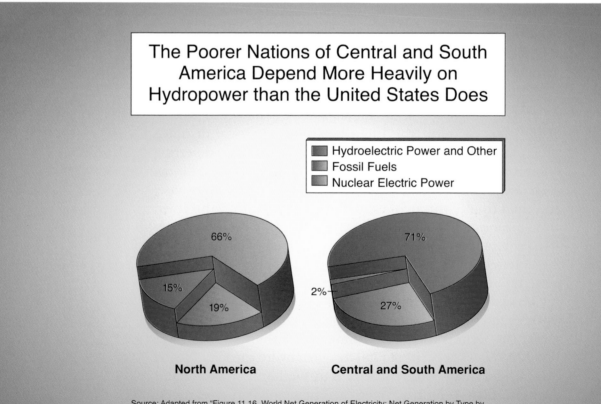

The Poorer Nations of Central and South America Depend More Heavily on Hydropower than the United States Does

- Hydroelectric Power and Other
- Fossil Fuels
- Nuclear Electric Power

66%

15%

19%

North America

71%

2%

27%

Central and South America

Source: Adapted from "Figure 11.16. World Net Generation of Electricity: Net Generation by Type by Region, 2002 (Percent of Regional Total)," in *Annual Energy Review 2003*, U.S. Department of Energy, Energy Information Administration, Office of Energy Markets and End Use, September 7, 2004. www.eia.doe.gov/emeu/aer/pdf/aer.pdf.

being divided among local people, rather than going to outside state agencies or companies.

Unfortunately there are many cases where the potential benefits of building small-hydro plants with local materials and know-how have been lost because the plants were built by highly paid foreign hydro engineers as smaller versions of large hydrodams, with unnecessarily complex and expensive designs and construction materials. Small dams and weirs made of rubble and wood may appear unacceptable to engineers accustomed to building in concrete and steel, but their temporary nature can be a benefit—when they are washed away so are the sediments behind them. Small hydro with temporary dams, weir diversions or reservoirs which are so small that it is practicable to clean out their accumulated sediments are, unlike most larger hydro plants, truly renewable technologies. . . .

Small Hydro Beats Large Hydro in Nepal

The successful campaign in the early 1990s against the $1 billion, 201 MW Arun III Dam in Nepal was started by Nepali small-hydro engineers who feared that Arun III would wipe out the country's growing small-hydro industry. Arun III would have been built almost exclusively by foreign contractors, and would have consumed virtually all the investment in the Nepali power sector for the next decade and more. The dam's opponents argued that small- and medium-sized dams could provide equivalent new generating capacity cheaper and quicker than Arun III: mini- and micro-schemes in Nepal commonly cost from $1,200 to $2,000 per instilled kilowatt, far less than the projected cost of $5,000 per kW for Arun III. Small-hydro plants can be completed in two to three years—Arun III would have taken more than a decade to build. The announcement in August 1995 that the World Bank would not fund the scheme, and would help to find alternative power sources, marked a significant victory for the proponents of small hydro in Nepal and elsewhere.

Small Hydro Can Be Harmful

While a single small-hydro project will have less environmental and social impacts than a large project in the same location, this does not mean that small hydro cannot be harmful. Small dams can have as serious an impact upon the flow patterns, chemistry and temperature of streams and small rivers as large dams can have upon large rivers. Small dams can significantly reduce numbers of migratory fish, especially when several are built on the same river. Weir and diversion micro-hydro projects can also harm aquatic species by dewatering the river between the canal intake and the tailrace.

Huge numbers of small-hydro plants can also cause the resettlement of huge numbers of people: according to government

A turbine generates electricity at a hydroelectric dam on the Danube River. Turbine placement and construction can help minimize environmental damage caused by dams.

statistics, 70 per cent of the 10 million people displaced by Chinese reservoirs lost their land due to 'small projects'. (No definition of 'small project' is given with these statistics. They presumably include many non-hydro reservoirs.) While these data are difficult to interpret and of dubious reliability, they do give an idea of the potential scale of the problem.

There are, however, a number of ways of increasing small-hydro capacity which avoid most environmental and resettlement problems. One is to install turbines in irrigation channels and municipal water supply and wastewater systems. The retrofitting of non-hydro small dams with turbines and the rehabilitation and upgrading of old small-hydro plants can in some cases increase generating capacity at little extra economic or environmental cost. Rehabilitation and upgrading (replacing old turbines and generators with more efficient modern equipment) now accounts for most of the current small-hydro development in Europe and North America. Adding capacity by upgrading small-hydro plants in the US is estimated to cost $200–$700 per kW, and adding turbines at an existing non-hydro dam $600–$2,500 per kW. A variant of small hydro which could be commercialized within the next decade is the 'free-flow' turbine—the underwater equivalent of a wind turbine. Groups of these turbines would be tethered to riverbeds or hung from barges and would not require dams or diversions.

3 Ocean Temperature Gradients Could Be Used to Generate Electricity

U.S. Department of Energy

In the following article the U.S. Department of Energy (DOE) explains how Ocean Thermal Energy Conversion (OTEC) could become an important power source. The OTEC process uses the heat energy stored in the ocean to generate electricity, according to the DOE. OTEC works best when the difference in temperature between the top, warmer layer and the bottom, colder layer of the ocean is large, conditions that exist in the tropics. In one type of OTEC system, warm seawater is placed in a low-pressure container, which causes the water to boil. The resulting steam powers a turbine attached to an electrical generator. The steam is then condensed back into a liquid by exposure to cold seawater. The DOE claims that OTEC could supply future energy needs if nations invest in improving conversion technology. The U.S. Department of Energy handles the nation's energy policies.

A process called Ocean Thermal Energy Conversion (OTEC) uses the heat energy stored in the Earth's oceans to generate electricity. OTEC works best when the temperature difference between the warmer, top layer of the ocean and

Energy Efficiency and Renewable Energy, U.S. Department of Energy, "A Consumer's Guide to Energy Efficiency and Renewable Energy: Ocean Thermal Energy Conversion," www.eere.energy.gov, September, 2005.

the colder, deep ocean water is about 20°C (36°F). These conditions exist in tropical coastal areas, roughly between the Tropic of Capricorn and the Tropic of Cancer. To bring the cold water to the surface, OTEC plants require an expensive, large diameter intake pipe, which is submerged a mile or more into the ocean's depths.

Some energy experts believe that if it could become cost-competitive with conventional power technologies, OTEC could produce billions of watts of electrical power.

History of Ocean Energy

OTEC technology is not new. In 1881, Jacques Arsene d'Arsonval, a French physicist, proposed tapping the thermal energy of the ocean. But it was d'Arsonval's student, Georges Claude, who in 1930 actually built the first OTEC plant in Cuba. The system produced 22 kilowatts of electricity with a low-pressure turbine. In 1935, Claude constructed another plant aboard a 10,000-ton cargo vessel moored off the coast of Brazil. Weather and waves destroyed both plants before they became net power generators. (Net power is the amount of power generated after subtracting power needed to run the system.)

In 1956, French scientists designed another 3-megawatt OTEC plant for Abidjan, Ivory Coast, West Africa. The plant was never completed, however, because it was too expensive.

The United States became involved in OTEC research in 1974 with the establishment of the Natural Energy Laboratory of Hawaii Authority. The Laboratory has become one of the world's leading test facilities for OTEC technology.

Three Types of OTEC Technology

The types of OTEC systems include the following:

- *Closed-Cycle*

  These systems use fluid with a low-boiling point, such as ammonia, to rotate a turbine to generate electricity. Warm surface seawater is pumped through a heat exchanger where the low-boiling-point fluid is vaporized. The expanding vapor turns the turbo-generator. Cold deep-seawater—pumped through a second heat exchanger

—condenses the vapor back into a liquid, which is then recycled through the system.

In 1979, the Natural Energy Laboratory and several private-sector partners developed the mini OTEC experiment, which achieved the first successful at-sea production of net electrical power from closed-cycle OTEC. The mini OTEC vessel was moored 1.5 miles (2.4 km) off the Hawaiian coast and produced enough net electricity to illuminate the ship's light bulbs and run its computers and televisions.

In 1999, the Natural Energy Laboratory tested a 250-kW pilot OTEC closed-cycle plant, the largest such plant ever put into operation.

- *Open-Cycle*

These systems use the tropical oceans' warm surface water to make electricity. When warm seawater is placed in a

The general manager of Xenesys energy systems shows off Ocean Thermal Energy Conversion (OTEC) technology at his Mauritius plant.

low-pressure container, it boils. The expanding steam drives a low-pressure turbine attached to an electrical generator. The steam, which has left its salt behind in the low-pressure container, is almost pure fresh water. It is condensed back into a liquid by exposure to cold temperatures from deep-ocean water.

In 1984, the Solar Energy Research Institute (now the National Renewable Energy Laboratory) developed a vertical-spout evaporator to convert warm seawater into low-pressure steam for open-cycle plants. Energy conversion efficiencies as high as 97% were achieved. In May 1993, an open-cycle OTEC plant at Keahole Point, Hawaii, produced 50,000 watts of electricity during a net power-producing experiment.

ANOTHER OPINION →

Between Warm and Cold Waters

"The temperature difference between the warm surface waters and the cold deep waters of the ocean represent a significant potential energy source."

Dan White, "Ocean Energy—Putting It All in Perspective," April 18, 2005. www.renewableenergyaccess.com.

- *Hybrid*

  These systems combine the features of both the closed-cycle and open-cycle systems. In a hybrid system, warm seawater enters a vacuum chamber where it is flash-evaporated into steam, similar to the open-cycle evaporation process. The steam vaporizes a low-boiling-point fluid (in a closed-cycle loop) that drives a turbine to produce electricity.

The Advantages of OTEC

OTEC has important benefits other than power production. For example, air conditioning can be a byproduct. Spent cold seawater from an OTEC plant can chill fresh water in a heat exchanger or flow directly into a cooling system. Simple systems of this type have air conditioned buildings at the Natural Energy Laboratory for several years.

OTEC technology also supports chilled-soil agriculture. When cold seawater flows through underground pipes, it chills the surrounding soil. The temperature difference between plant roots in the cool soil and plant leaves in the warm air allows

Ocean Temperature Difference Between Surface and Depth of 3,280 Feet

Longitude

| Less than 64.4°F | 68° to 71.6°F | More than 75°F |
| 64.4° to 68°F | 71.6° to 75°F | Depth less than 3,280 feet |

Source: National Renewable Energy Laboratory, "What Is Ocean Thermal Energy Conversion?" May 2006. www.nrel.gov.

many plants that evolved in temperate climates to be grown in the subtropics. The Natural Energy Laboratory maintains a demonstration garden near its OTEC plant with more than 100 different fruits and vegetables, many of which would not normally survive in Hawaii.

Aquaculture is perhaps the most well-known byproduct of OTEC. Cold-water delicacies, such as salmon and lobster, thrive in the nutrient-rich, deep seawater from the OTEC process. Microalgae such as Spirulina, a health food supplement, also can be cultivated in the deep-ocean water.

As mentioned earlier, another advantage of open or hybrid-cycle OTEC plants is the production of fresh water from seawater. Theoretically, an OTEC plant that generates 2-MW of net electricity could produce about 4,300 cubic meters (14,118.3 cubic feet) of desalinated water each day.

OTEC also may one day provide a means to mine ocean water for 57 trace elements. Most economic analyses have suggested that mining the ocean for dissolved substances would be unprofitable. Mining involves pumping large volumes of water and the expense of separating the minerals from seawater. But with OTEC plants already pumping the water, the only remaining economic challenge is to reduce the cost of the extraction process.

Environmental and Economic Challenges

In general, careful site selection is the key to keeping the environmental impacts of OTEC to a minimum. OTEC experts believe that appropriate spacing of plants throughout the tropical oceans can nearly eliminate any potential negative impacts of OTEC processes on ocean temperatures and on marine life.

OTEC power plants require substantial capital investment upfront. OTEC researchers believe private sector firms probably will be unwilling to make the enormous initial investment required to build large-scale plants until the price of fossil fuels increases dramatically or until national governments provide financial incentives. Another factor hindering the commercialization of OTEC is that there are only a few hundred land-based sites in the tropics where deep-ocean water is close enough to shore to make OTEC plants feasible.

Ocean Waves Could Become an Important Energy Source

4

Energy Systems Research Unit

Using the power of ocean waves to generate electricity has enormous potential, the Energy Systems Research Unit (ESRU) asserts in the following article. One type of wave energy collector that the ESRU describes consists of a cylinder floating on the ocean's surface. As waves roll under it, the cylinder rotates, turning a turbine attached to an electrical generator. Another type of collector uses a loosely segmented platform floating on the surface of the sea. As the device moves with the waves, the movement of the joints is used to drive a turbine. A third wave collection device works by trapping seawater in a column-shaped vessel; as the sea undulates, the water within the column acts like a piston to pump air, driving a turbine. The Energy Systems Research Unit is located at the University of Strathclyde in Glasgow, Scotland.

Waves are a result of the effects of wind on the oceans and seas. This wind originates from the major influx of energy to this planet: solar energy from the sun. The energy contained within waves around the world is huge; in some places values of 70MW/km [megawatts/kilometers] of wave front are experienced. In theory it could then be said that huge generating stations could be built which would capture all this energy

Energy Systems Research Unit, "Wave Power," June 2002. www.esru.strath.ac.uk. Used by permission.

and supply all or most of our needs. But there are many factors affecting this kind of deployment. . . .

Waves are not as consistent as the tide and therefore there is a definite problem with matching supply and demand. This is one of the main reasons that wave power has so far been restricted to small scale schemes; no large scale commercial plant is in action.

Identifying areas of suitable wave height is something that has to be done before deployment can start. The highest concentration of wave power is found in the windiest areas, which are mainly between latitudes 40 and 60 in both northern and southern hemispheres. . . . The technology must be able to withstand the freak wave heights that can be experienced, in rough and remote locations where access can be difficult.

Three Types of Wave Power

There are three main categories [of] wave power: Near Shore, At Shore and Off Shore. There are obvious environmental and social considerations to go with . . . these conditions.

Near Shore operations have to consider the aesthetic influence they will have on what could be a picturesque area. They also will have a definite impact on shipping and marine life, but . . . this will be no greater than current offshore installations. It has been suggested that a distance of 12 miles from shore is the distance within which a device is said to be near shore. . . .

On shore wave power will have a marked effect on the area [in which] it is deployed. There are ways of incorporating [wave facilities] into existing structures to minimise the effect, such as harbour walls. . . .

Wave Energy Collector Technology

There are three types of wave energy collectors. These are:

- Buoyant Moored Device
- Hinged Contour Device
- Oscillating Water Column

The Buoyant Moored Device
This type of device floats on the surface of the water or below it. It is moored to the seabed by either a taut or loose mooring

system. One example of this type of device . . . , the Edinburgh or Salter Duck, [will be discussed]. . . .

Ducks work by independently rotating about a long linkage; this maintains [the device's] stability by out spanning wave crests. The front edge of the duck matches the wave particle motion. In moderate seas, the more cylindrical back portion creates no stern waves but when the weather is bad these parts shed energy through wave making to the rear. The device requires a

George Taylor is the president of Ocean Power Technologies, a company that develops ways to convert the energy of ocean waves into electricity.

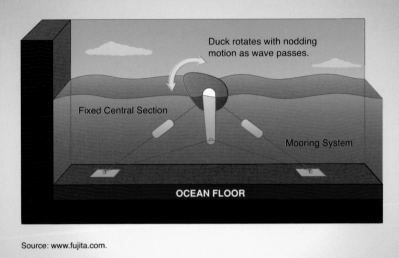

The Duck Wave Energy Collector

Duck rotates with nodding motion as wave passes.

Fixed Central Section

Mooring System

OCEAN FLOOR

Source: www.fujita.com.

depth of at least 80 metres and uses a system of weights and floats to give almost constant tension in the mooring cables.

Hinged Contour Device

This type of device follows the motion of the waves; it creates power using the motion at the joints. It is commonly moored slackly to hold it in place. One such device is known as the Pelamis.

As the Pelamis moves with the waves, the motion is resisted at the joints by hydraulic rams that pump high-pressure oil through hydraulic motors via smoothing accumulators. These motors are used to drive generators to create power. It has been said that a 750kW device would be 150m long and 3.5m in diameter and comprise five sections.

Oscillating Water Column (OWC)

This method of generating power from the tide works by using a column of water as a piston to pump air and drive a turbine to generate power. This type of device can be fixed to the seabed or installed on shore. . . .

The Economics of Wave Power

At present, the main stumbling block to deployment of wave energy devices is funding. . . . The capital costs are the problem,

Wave Energy as a Renewable Source

"Wave energy has been hailed as the most promising renewable source for maritime countries. It does no environmental damage and is inexhaustible—the waves go on forever."

David Ross, *Our Planet*, 2001.

as it is hard to get companies to invest in technologies that have not yet been completely proved. Similar to other forms of renewable energy sources such as wind and solar, the fuel is free for the complete lifetime of the scheme.

Wave devices that are on-shore have social implications for the surrounding area. They can be integrated within harbour walls, which can affect shipping and cause noise pollution. They can create employment in the area and attract visitors.

Offshore devices have an effect on navigation, and consultation with affected bodies must be undertaken. The experiences of other offshore industries, such as oil, should aid this part of planning for wave devices.

There can be environmental impacts resulting from wave powered devices. But, like other renewables, these impacts must be compared to the effects of fossil or nuclear generation. Devices that are on-shore can have environmental benefits, such as helping to reduce the erosion of the landscape. Any devices off shore can have an effect on the aquatic life in that area, but this again is very site specific and hard to predict. But anchoring systems can become almost like artificial reefs, creating a place for new colonisation.

Facts About Water

The Chemical Composition of Water (H₂O)

In 1860 scientist Stanislao Cannizzaro determined that the chemical composition of water consists of two hydrogen atoms and one oxygen atom. Water is the most abundant substance on Earth, covering more than 70 percent of the planet. Because it continually renews itself through the hydrologic cycle (evaporation followed by precipitation), water is considered a renewable resource. Of all the available renewable resources—including water, solar, wind, geothermal, and biomass—water (utilized in hydroelectric facilities) is the most widely used.

How Electricity Is Generated Using Water Power

The kinetic energy of moving water can be converted to electricity. In hydroelectric applications, falling water is used to generate electricity. Typically, water is stored behind a dam in a reservoir. When electricity is needed, water is released from the reservoir into a penstock, which diverts the torrent to a turbine. When the water rushes over the turbine, its blades turn, powering a generator. The electricity is then routed to cities via transmission lines. Wave power takes advantage of the fact that when the ocean meets land, waves are produced. Devices that float on the surface of the water rotate as waves pass under them, turning a turbine. The larger the waves, the more energy potential there is. Tidal power uses the energy created when sea levels rise and fall with the tides. To harness this power, a tidal dam is built across an estuary or other narrow inlet. When sea levels rise at high tide, dam gates are opened, letting the water flow into a chamber. The water pushes up air, which acts as a piston to turn a turbine.

Types of Dams

arch dam: Built to curve into the reservoir that fills behind it. This arch shape gives the dam extra strength. The curve of the dam makes it stronger by spreading the weight of the water through the whole wall and into the ground at the sides.

gravity dam: Usually a huge wall of concrete that is wider at the bottom than at the top. This design allows the dam to hold back the weight of the water pushing on it from the accompanying reservoir.

embankment dam: Made of earth and/or rock in a triangle shape that allows it to withstand the weight of the water behind it. To withstand this weight, embankment dams are built so that the bottom is at least four times as wide as the top. An embankment dam also needs a waterproof layer of earth and rock, either on the outside face of the dam or on the inside to keep the water from leaching through.

buttress dam: A solid wall of concrete, with a solid face that the reservoir water rests against. The wall is supported by triangular-shaped buttresses behind that keep the dam from falling over from the weight of the water pushing against it. All dam designs are wider at the bottom than they are at the top. This is because the pressure of the water at the bottom of the reservoir is much greater than the pressure of the water at the top. How strong the dam needs to be depends on how deep the reservoir will be that fills behind it.

Sizes of Hydropower Installations

- **Micro** hydropower systems produce small amounts of electricity (up to one hundred kilowatts). A micro system can produce enough power to run a home or farm.
- **Small** hydropower systems produce enough electricity (one hundred kilowatts to thirty megawatts) to run a ranch complex or a small town.
- **Large** hydropower systems can produce enough electricity (more than thirty megawatts) to run large industrial complexes and meet the electricity needs of large cities.

How Electricity Is Measured

A watt-hour is a unit of measure for electric power. One watt is one watt of power used for one hour. For example, a 100-watt lightbulb uses 100 watt-hours of power in one hour.

1 kilowatt-hour (kWh) = 1000 watts

1 megawatt-hour (MWh) = 1000 kWh

1 gigawatt-hour (GWh) = 1000 MWh

1 terawatt-hour (TWh) = 1000 GWh

Types of Hydropower Generation Facilities

- **An impoundment** facility uses a dam to block the flow of a river, resulting in a reservoir. The water from the reservoir is released in a regulated way to turn the turbines inside the dam, which power a generator to produce electricity. The reservoir water can be released at whatever rate is needed by the facility to meet power needs.

- **Diversion** facilities, also called run-of-river projects, use the natural flow of a river to produce electricity; they do not usually require a dam. The river is usually channeled through a penstock or canal to generate the flow needed to turn a turbine.

- **Pumped storage** facilities move water from a lower reservoir to a higher reservoir when demand for electricity is low. When demand rises, the water is released from the upper reservoir to flow down to the lower one. The force of gravity causes the water to flow rapidly, which turns the blades of a turbine.

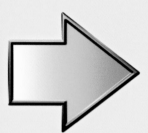

Glossary

acre-foot: Used to measure water quantity in a reservoir. An acre-foot is the volume of water one foot deep, covering one acre. One acre equals 43,560 square feet.

baseload power: The amount of power that a utility company has to generate on a regular basis.

capacity: The amount of power that can be generated by any power-generating facility.

clean energy: A source of energy that does not have any waste products or waste gases that pollute the surrounding environment.

dam: A wall, usually made of concrete or dirt, that holds back the water of a river or stream. Some dams can be opened or closed to control water flow.

electricity: A form of energy created by the flow of electrons. Electricity can be used to produce light, heat, or motion.

fish ladders: Passageways that allow fish to pass through dams on their way upstream to spawn.

generator: A machine in which mechanical energy is turned into electric energy. For hydroelectric applications, generators receive mechanical energy from the turning blades of turbines, which are powered by moving water.

head height: The distance in height from the turbines (in a power plant or dam) to the surface of the water being used. This height, along with the amount of water being used, determines how much power can be generated by the hydroelectric facility. Generally, the greater the head height, the more electricity can be generated.

horizontal waterwheel: A waterwheel powered by the forward action of flowing water.

hydroelectric: Refers to the generation of electricity from the power of water. This power generation can be accomplished using dams (hydropower), waves (wave power), or the tides (tidal power).

hydrokinetic: Refers to using the energy of moving water—usually streams, rivers, tidal estuaries, and constructed waterways—without the use of water diversion or dams, to generate power.

hydrologic cycle: The process of evaporation and precipitation. Water evaporates from lakes and oceans, forms clouds, falls back to land as snow or rain, and flows back into lakes and oceans.

hydropower: The energy of moving water converted into electricity. The amount of electricity that is generated depends on water flow and the head height.

kilowatt: An electrical power unit of measure equal to one thousand watts.

land-based OTEC: Ocean thermal energy conversion systems that are located on shore (see ocean thermal energy conversion).

near-shore OTEC: Ocean thermal energy conversion systems that are mounted on the ocean shelf (see ocean thermal energy conversion).

ocean thermal energy conversion (OTEC): The conversion of thermal or heat energy from the oceans into electricity. In some applications warmer water from the top layer of the ocean is pressured, producing steam to turn a turbine. Then, cool water from the ocean bottom is used to chill the steam back to water, which is pumped back into the ocean. The process often produces desalinized water as a byproduct.

offshore OTEC: Ocean thermal energy conversion systems that are floating in the ocean (see ocean thermal energy conversion).

overshot waterwheel: A waterwheel powered by water flowing over the top of the wheel, making the wheel turn.

penstock: The pipe in a dam that carries water from the reservoir to the turbines.

power output: The amount of power generated from the water flowing through the turbines of a hydroelectric facility.

reservoir: A place behind a dam where the river water is held and stored. The water in a reservoir can be used to make electricity when demand for power is high. It can also hold water from rain and winter snows to be used during times of little precipitation.

salinity: The amount of salt in ocean water.

tidal power: Power generated from the rise and fall of the ocean tides.

turbidity: The amount of sediment that is churned up in water.

turbine: A rotary engine that uses kinetic energy (such as that contained in the flow of water) to create mechanical energy. Turbines often power generators, which produce electricity.

undershot waterwheel: A vertical waterwheel placed in the middle of a stream. The flow of the water turns the wheel's blades, producing power.

water mill: Mills that use the power of moving water to drive grinding stones.

waterwheel: An apparatus that uses falling or flowing water to create power.

watt: A measure of electrical power. One watt is equal to the work done at the rate of one joule per second or equal to the power produced by a current of one ampere across a potential difference of one volt.

wave power: The energy of ocean waves harnessed to generate electricity.

weir: A low dam that has been built to hold back the water of a stream or river, usually for a mill.

Chronology

B.C.

3000
A water supply system using dams is built in what is now Jordan.

2600
Building on a dam begins in Egypt at the time of the first pyramids. The dam was partially washed away and was never completed.

250
First recorded use of waterpower, which was used to run a clock.

100
Greeks use waterwheels for grinding wheat.

A.D. 1700s
Modern hydropower begins with the publication of *Architecture Hydraulique* by French engineer Bernard Forest de Belidor.

1800s
European and American factories use the waterwheel to power their machines.

1829
Lester Pelton invents the Pelton Wheel, also known as the Pelton turbine. In this design the water hits the side of the water cup, instead of the middle, and this makes the wheel (turbine) move faster.

1832
Benoit Fourneyron, a French engineer, perfects the first water turbine.

1839
Lorenzo Adkins patents a waterwheel.

1874
The first recorded dam failure in the United States occurs on Mill Creek, a tributary of the Connecticut River, killing 143 people.

1880
The Grand Rapids Electric Light and Power Company in Michigan generates electricity with a water turbine and lights up eighteen Brush arc lamps; Lester Pelton receives his first patent for a water turbine.

1881
Hydropower is used to light city street lamps in Niagara Falls, New York; that hydroelectric site is still in use today.

1882
The first U.S. hydroelectric plant is built in Appleton, Wisconsin; it utilizes a run-of-river dam.

1886
Fifty water-powered electric plants are either running or under construction in the United States.

1887
The first hydroelectric plant in the western United States is built in San Bernardino, California.

1889
Two hundred electric plants use water for power generation; a dam above Johnstown, Pennsylvania, collapses, killing twenty-two hundred people.

1893
The first dam built specifically for hydropower is completed in Austin, Texas, on the Colorado River.

1902
Congress passes the National Reclamation Act. This act sets up the Reclamation Service, which is to be in charge of bringing water to the arid lands of the western United States.

1907
Fifteen percent of U.S. electricity is generated with hydro-power.

1920

Twenty-five percent of U.S. electricity is generated with hydropower. The Federal Power Act establishes the Federal Power Commission; this commission issues licenses for hydroelectric development on public lands.

1928

St. Francis Dam fails in California; more than 350 are killed.

1930

The first OTEC plant is constructed in Cuba.

1931

Construction begins on Boulder Dam (later known as Hoover Dam).

1933

Construction begins on Grand Coulee Dam and Bonneville Dam on the Columbia River in Washington State.

1935

Boulder Dam (later known as Hoover Dam) is dedicated by President Franklin D. Roosevelt.

1937

Bonneville Dam, the first federal dam, begins operation.

1940

Forty percent of U.S. electricity is generated with hydropower. There are over fifteen hundred hydroelectric facilities producing power.

1963

Construction on Glen Canyon Dam on the Arizona-Utah border is completed, creating Lake Powell, which eventually ends up almost two hundred miles long.

1968

The Wild and Scenic Rivers Act excludes protected rivers from consideration as hydropower sites.

1972

Rapid City, South Dakota, receives fourteen inches of rain in six hours on June 9; Canyon Lake Dam on Rapid Creek gives way, killing more than two hundred people.

1974
The U.S. government begins OTEC research at the National Energy Laboratory in Hawaii.

1990s
The U.S. Department of Energy begins research and development of advanced hydropower technology in an effort to generate more electricity with less environmental impact.

2000
The top five hydroelectric producing countries are Canada, the United States, Brazil, Russia, and China, in that order.

2002
The U.S. Army Corps of Engineers National Inventory of Dams contains over seventy-five thousand entries. Only 3 percent of these dams are for hydroelectric purposes.

2003
Roughly 10 percent of U.S. electricity is generated with hydropower.

2006
The U.S. Department of Energy estimates that there are over fifty-six hundred undeveloped hydropower sites in this country; over 50 percent of these sites already have some type of dam or other structure on them that does not generate electric power.

For Further Reading

Books, Papers, and Fact Sheets

Michael Collier, Robert H. Webb, and John C. Schmidt, *Dams and Rivers: Primer on the Downstream Effects of Dams*. Washington, DC: U.S. Geological Survey, June 1996.

Francis and Joseph Gies, *Cathedral, Forge, and Waterwheel Technology and Invention in the Middle Ages*. New York: Harper-Collins, 1994.

Elizabeth Grossman, *Watershed: The Undamming of America*. New York: Counterpoint, 2002.

Jacques Leslie, *Deep Water: The Epic Struggle Over Dams, Displaced People, and the Environment*. New York: Farrar, Straus, and Giroux, 2005.

Patrick McCully, *Silenced Rivers: The Ecology and Politics of Large Dams*. London: Zed, 2001.

National Hydropower Association, *Outstanding Stewardship of America's Rivers Report*, April 2006. www.hydro.org.

Fred Pearce, *When the Rivers Run Dry: Water—The Defining Crisis of the Twenty-First Century*. Boston: Beacon, 2006.

John W. Simpson, *Dam! Water, Power, Politics, and Preservation in Hetch Hetchy and Yosemite National Park*. New York: Pantheon Books, 2005.

Patrick Takahashi and Andrew Trenka, *Ocean Thermal Energy Conversion*. New York: John Wiley, 1996.

Periodicals

Edna Francisco, "Tales of the Undammed," *Science News*, April 10, 2004.

Ken Garcia, "The Hetch Hetchy Pipe Dream," *San Francisco Chronicle*, August 5, 2005.

Dundan Graham-Rowe, "Hydro's Dirty Secret Revealed," *New Scientist*, February 26, 2005.

John W. Keys III, "The Colorado River System: Dams and Drought," *Salt Lake Tribune*, September 10, 2005.

Oliver Klaus, "Hydropower Comes into Its Own," *Meed*, August 2, 2002.

Gregory Mone, "Making Better Surf and Cleaner Power," *Popular Science*, February 2006.

Stephen J. Mraz, "Plugging into the Ocean," *Machine Design*, September 16, 2004.

Paul Ostapuk, "Guest Opinion: Thank Heaven We Have Lakes Powell, Mead," *Tucson Citizen*, September 8, 2005.

Kenneth H. Reckhow, "A Better Way to Clean Up the Nation's Waters," *Popular Mechanics*, August 28, 2001.

"Special Report: Safeguarding Our Water," *Scientific American*, February 2001.

Alex Shoumatoff, "Who Owns This River?" *OnEarth*, Spring 2005.

Lisa Stiffler and Robert McClure, "Our Warming World: Effects of Climate Change Bode Ill for Northwest," *Seattle Post-Intelligencer*, November 13, 2003.

Patrick Symmes, "River Impossible," *Outside*, August 2003.

Mark Taugher, "Bruce Babbitt Calls for More Dams to Cope with Global Warming's Effects," *Contra Costa Times*, August 29, 2005.

Internet Sources

Mary Bellis, "How Tidal Power Plants Work," *About*, 2006. www.about.com.

Staffan Bergtsson, "Sweden's Renewable Energy Resources," Sweden. SE, June 2004. www.sweden.se.

Chad Boutin, "Fuel Cells Might Get Hydrogen from Water, Organic Material," *Purdue News*, August 31, 2005. www.news. uns.purdue.edu.

Andy Darvill, "Wave Power—Energy from the Wind on the Sea," Claranet, December 10, 2005. http://home.clara.net/ darvill/altenergy/wave.htm.

Foundation for Water and Energy Education, "About Hydropower," 2002. www.fwee.org/abhydro.html.

Theodore R. Hazen, "A History of the Water Wheel," Angelfire, April 2002. www.angelfire.com/journal/millbuilder/ historical.html.

Lenntech, "Water Energy FAQ," 2006. www.lenntech.com.

LSA Research Group, "What Is Hydropower?" 2003. www. lsa. colorado.edu.

Katrina Lyon and Mark McHenry, "Tidal Energy Systems," Renewable Energy Systems Test Center, 2006. www.reslab.com. au/resfiles/tidal/text.html.

Hillary Mayell, "UN Highlights World Water Crisis," *National Geographic News*, June 5, 2003. www.nationalgeographic.com.

National Hydropower Association, "NHA Forecast for Hydropower Development Through 2020," 2006. www.hydro. org/hydro facts/forecast.asp.

Christopher Peterson, "Save the Restored Cathedral in the Desert and Fort Moquil," Rivers Foundation of the Americas, 2004. www.riversfoundation.org.

Probe International, "China to Prevent Pollution, Increase Hydropower at Mekong River," February 21, 2001. www. probe internationl.org.

Stewart Ridgway, "Out of Gas? Refuel with Mist Lift Ocean Thermal Energy," *OTECnews*, April 19, 2005. www. otecnews.org/articles/mistlift.html.

Emily Rudkin, "Marine Current Energy," WEC Survey of Energy Resources, 2001. www.worldenergy.org.

Sea Solar Power Inc., "Power and Fresh Water from the Sun Via the Sea." www.seasolarpower.com/otec.html.

Sustainable Energy Coalition, "Hydropower Technologies," 2000. www.sustainableenergy.org.

U.S. Bureau of Reclamation, "The History of Hydropower Development in the United States," October 2004. www.usbr.gov/power/edu/history.html.

U.S. Department of Energy, "Ocean Thermal Energy Conversion," September 2005. www.eere.energy.gov.

Dan White, "Ocean Energy—Putting It All in Perspective," *Renewable Energy Access*, April 18, 2005. www.renewableenergyaccess.com.

Web Sites

National Hydropower Association (NHA) (www.hydro.org). This nonprofit trade association promotes the use of hydropower as a clean, renewable, safe energy resource for the United States. The NHA Web site includes information such as fact sheets, news briefs, and research reports.

U.S. Bureau of Reclamation (www.usbr.gov.). The Bureau of Reclamation is part of the U.S. Department of the Interior. Its Web site covers all aspects of water management, including dams and reservoirs, and other hydroelectric facilities. The site makes available news briefs, water related databases, hydroelectric history, and fact sheets.

U.S. Department of Energy (www.eere.energy.gov). The Department of Energy Web site provides a variety of information concerning hydropower in the United States. The Energy Efficiency and Renewable Energy branch provides information on hydropower facilities, wave and tidal power, statistics on hydropower, information on the advantages and disadvantages of hydropower, and information on the most recent advances in hydropower research and development.

Index

Picture Credits

Cover, Getty Images
Associated Press, AP, 13, 71, 73, 78, 98
© Bettmann/CORBIS, 41
© Andrew Brown; Ecoscene/CORBIS, 40
© W. Cody/CORBIS, 16
© Joel Creed; Ecoscene/CORBIS, 62
© Sean Daveys/Australian Picture Library/CORBIS, 14
© Rick Doyle/CORBIS, 27
© Natalie Fobes/CORBIS, 47, 81
© Robert Harding/World Imagery/CORBIS, 68
© Blaine Harrington III/CORBIS, 11
© Chris Hellier/CORBIS, 56
© Collart Herve/CORBIS SYGMA, 57
© Images/Corbis, 37
© Larry Lee Photography/CORBIS, 32
© Attar Maher/CORBIS SYGMA, 20
© Kevin R. Morrris/CORBIS, 85
© Negri, Brescia/CORBIS, 24
© David Stephenson/CORBIS, 45
© Stuart Westmoreland/CORBIS, 60
AFP/Getty Images, 92
Time Life Pictures/Getty Images, 88
Rogulin Dmitry/ITAR-Tass/Landov, 24
Library of Congress, 21
North Wind Picture Archives, 18
Steve Zmina, 39, 43, 54, 65, 67, 77, 86, 94, 99

About the Editor

Carrie Fredericks received her BA from Detroit's Wayne State University, majoring in English and minoring in general science studies. She has worked on Thomson/Gale publications for 15 years. This is her first publication for Greenhaven Press. She resides, with her family, in Michigan.